Succeed Every Day

Daily Readings for Teens

PAMELA ESPELAND

free spirit
PUBLISHING®

Works for kids®

Copyright © 2001 by Pamela Espeland

All rights reserved under International and Pan-American Copyright
Conventions. Unless otherwise noted, no part of this book may be
reproduced, stored in a retrieval system, or transmitted in any form
or by any means, electronic, mechanical, photocopying, recording, or
otherwise, without express written permission of the publisher,
except for brief quotations or critical reviews.

Library of Congress Cataloging-in-Publication Data
Espeland, Pamela
    Succeed every day : daily readings for teens / Pamela Espeland.
       p. cm.
    Includes indexes.
    ISBN 1-57542-083-X (pbk.)
    1. Teenagers—Conduct of life—Juvenile literature. 2. Self-
actualization (Psychology) in adolescence—Juvenile literature. [1.
Conduct of life. 2. Self-actualization (Psychology)] I. Title.

HQ796 .E684 2001
158.1'0835—dc21   00-052815

10 9 8 7 6 5 4 3 2 1
Printed in the United States of America

The framework of developmental assets that is the basis for this book is
used under a license from Search Institute, 700 S. Third St., Suite 210,
Minneapolis, MN 55415. Copyright © 1997 by Search Institute. For information, visit the Web site (www.search-institute.org).

Cover and book design: Marieka Heinlen
Assistant editor: KaTrina Wentzel
Subjects index: Randl Ockey

Free Spirit Publishing Inc.
217 Fifth Avenue North, Suite 200
Minneapolis, MN 55401-1299
(612) 338-2068
help4kids@freespirit.com
www.freespirit.com

The following are registered trademarks
of Free Spirit Publishing Inc.:

FREE SPIRIT®
FREE SPIRIT PUBLISHING®
SELF-HELP FOR TEENS®
SELF-HELP FOR KIDS®   free spirit
WORKS FOR KIDS®   PUBLISHING®
THE FREE SPIRITED CLASSROOM®

To Judy,
for 16 years and counting

Contents

Introduction

After you wake up in the morning, before you eat breakfast or even before you get out of bed, take a minute or two for the daily reading in *Succeed Every Day*. You might think of it as a gift you give yourself. A jump-starter for your brain.

Each reading begins with a quotation by somebody famous or not so famous (you'll recognize some of the names). Then there's a brief essay that relates to the quotation. The essay might give you a new perspective or an idea for something to try. Some essays tell stories about real people. Some give you contact information for organizations you might want to learn more about. Some will reinforce things you already know or believe; some might challenge your thinking. After the essay comes an affirmation—a short "Today I'll..." statement that suggests something you might do, consider, reflect on, plan, or ponder as you go about the rest of your day.

At the bottom of each page are words that won't make any sense at first. They might look like this:

Support
Asset #3: Other Adult Relationships

or this:

Social Competencies
Asset #34: Cultural Competence

These words are where this book began, so it's worth knowing what they mean.

All of the readings in *Succeed Every Day* are related to things called "developmental assets." The assets were identified and defined by Search Institute, a Minneapolis-based organization that specializes in research on children and teenagers. There are 40 assets, starting with #1: Family Support and continuing through #40: Positive View of Personal Future. The assets are grouped into eight categories. Support and Social Competencies are two of the categories.

And that's the most boring paragraph you'll have to read about the assets. Here's where it gets interesting.

Over the past 10 years, Search Institute has surveyed more than 1 million students in grades 6–12 in thousands of communities across the United States. When they study the survey results, they always see something with the power to change your life. Specifically: The *more* assets young people have, the *fewer* risky, dangerous things they do, and the *less* likely they are to get into trouble.

Assets seem to protect kids and teens from making choices that can hurt them. Assets also seem to empower kids and teens to make choices that can help them grow in positive, healthy ways. Some examples from surveys:

- 42 percent of kids and teens with 0–10 assets use drugs. Only 1 percent of kids and teens with 31–40 assets do.

- 43 percent of kids and teens with 0–10 assets have school problems. Only 2 percent of kids and teens with 31–40 assets do.

- 40 percent of kids and teens with 0–10 assets are often depressed and/or have attempted suicide. That number falls to 4 percent of kids and teens with 31–40 assets.

- 25 percent of kids and teens with 0–10 assets care about staying healthy. That number rises to 88 percent of kids and teens with 31–40 assets.

- 34 percent of kids and teens with 0–10 assets value diversity. They think it's important to know people of other racial/ethnic groups. That number jumps to 87 percent of kids and teens with 31–40 assets.

- 7 percent of kids and teens with 0–10 assets get mostly A's in school. Compare that to 53 percent of kids and teens with 31–40 assets.

So what do assets do? They form a solid foundation for your life. They have a positive influence on the choices you make and the actions you take. They help you become more competent, caring, and responsible. They keep you from getting involved in risky behaviors. They make you a better, stronger, wiser person—someone other people look up to, count on, trust, and respect. Assets are good things to have in your life and in yourself. You want them. You need them. You can get them.

The readings in *Succeed Every Day* help you build all 40 assets. The assets are named on the daily pages, but not defined. Here are the definitions.

Support Assets

#1: FAMILY SUPPORT. You feel loved and supported in your family.

#2: Positive Family Communication. You can go to your parents* for advice and support. You talk with each other often about many different topics—including serious issues.

#3: Other Adult Relationships. You know at least three adults (besides your parents) you can go to for advice and support. You talk with each other often about many different topics—including serious issues.

#4: Caring Neighborhood. You have neighbors who support you, encourage you, and care about you.

#5: Caring School Climate. Your school is a caring, encouraging place to be.

#6: Parent Involvement in Schooling. Your parents are actively involved in helping you succeed in school. They talk with you about school, sometimes help with your schoolwork, and attend school events.

---

*THE SMALL PRINT: When you see the word "parents" in this book, it means the adults you live with who take care of you. It's possible that you don't have two parents or even one. You might live with one or more stepparents, foster parents, grandparents, other relatives, or guardians. It's shorter and simpler to write "Talk to your parents…" than to write "Talk to your parent, stepparent, foster parent, grandparent, other relative, or guardian…." So please don't feel left out by the word "parents" if it isn't literally true for you.

Empowerment Assets

#7: COMMUNITY VALUES YOUTH. You feel that the adults in your community value and appreciate young people.

#8: YOUTH AS RESOURCES. You and other young people are given useful roles and meaningful things to do in your community.

#9: SERVICE TO OTHERS. You do an hour or more of community service each week.

#10: SAFETY. You feel safe at home, at school, and in your neighborhood.

Boundaries and Expectations Assets

#11: FAMILY BOUNDARIES. Your family has both clear rules and consequences for your behavior. They also monitor your whereabouts.

#12: SCHOOL BOUNDARIES. Your school has clear rules and consequences for behavior.

#13: NEIGHBORHOOD BOUNDARIES. Your neighbors take responsibility for monitoring your behavior.

#14: ADULT ROLE MODELS. Your parents and other adults in your life model positive, responsible behavior.

#15: POSITIVE PEER INFLUENCE. Your best friends model responsible behavior. They are a good influence on you. They do well at school, and they don't do risky things like drink alcohol or use other drugs.

#16: HIGH EXPECTATIONS. Your parents and teachers encourage you to do well.

Constructive Use of Time Assets

#17: CREATIVE ACTIVITIES. You spend three or more hours each week in lessons or practice in music, theater, or other arts.

#18: YOUTH PROGRAMS. You spend three or more hours each week in sports, clubs, or organizations at school and/or in the community.

#19: RELIGIOUS COMMUNITY. You spend one or more hours each week in religious services or spiritual activities.

#20: TIME AT HOME. You go out with friends with nothing special to do two or fewer nights each week.

Commitment to Learning Assets

#21: ACHIEVEMENT MOTIVATION. You want to do well in school.

#22: SCHOOL ENGAGEMENT. You like to learn new things.

#23: HOMEWORK. You do at least one hour of homework every school day.

#24: BONDING TO SCHOOL. You care about your school.

#25: READING FOR PLEASURE. You spend three or more hours each week reading for pleasure.

Positive Values Assets

#26: CARING. You believe that it's really important to help other people.

#27: EQUALITY AND SOCIAL JUSTICE. You want to help promote equality and reduce world poverty and hunger.

#28: INTEGRITY. You act on your convictions and stand up for your beliefs.

#29: HONESTY. You tell the truth—even when it's not easy.

#30: RESPONSIBILITY. You accept and take personal responsibility for your actions and decisions.

#31: RESTRAINT. You believe that it's important not to be sexually active or to use alcohol or other drugs.

Social Competencies Assets

#32: PLANNING AND DECISION MAKING. You know how to plan ahead and make choices.

#33: INTERPERSONAL COMPETENCE. You're good at making and keeping friends.

#34: CULTURAL COMPETENCE. You know and are comfortable with people of different cultural, racial, and/or ethnic backgrounds.

#35: RESISTANCE SKILLS. You resist negative peer pressure and avoid dangerous situations.

#36: PEACEFUL CONFLICT RESOLUTION. You try to resolve conflicts nonviolently.

Positive Identity Assets

#37: PERSONAL POWER. You feel that you have control over many things that happen to you.

#38: SELF-ESTEEM. You feel good about yourself.

#39: SENSE OF PURPOSE. You believe that your life has a purpose.

#40: POSITIVE VIEW OF PERSONAL FUTURE. You're optimistic about your future.

You may want to refer to these definitions every once in a while to learn which asset you're working on that day. Or not. It doesn't really matter. You don't have to know how the Internet works to check your email. It just works. You don't have to know that if you choose to hang out with your parents on February 27, you're building Asset #1: Family Support. You just are.

If you want to learn more about the developmental assets, visit Search Institute's Web site (www.search-institute.org). Or check out a book called *What Teens Need to Succeed: Proven, Practical Ways to Shape Your Own Future*, which includes more than 1,200 ideas for building assets at home, at school, in your community, in your congregation, and with your friends. For more information, contact Free Spirit Publishing (www.freespirit.com).

> "Each day comes bearing its own gifts.
> Untie the ribbons."
> *Ruth Ann Schabacker*

January 1

"Each day of your life, as soon as you open your eyes in the morning, you can square away for a happy and successful day."
George Matthew Adams

It's the first day of a brand new year. A fresh start. No reason not to be confident and hopeful. If last year didn't go the way you wanted, that was then and this is now. Start today with a positive attitude. If you're already in a good mood, great. If you're not, what can you do? Who can you call? Where can you go? Maybe you'll ring in the New Year with your family. Or hang out with friends. Or spend time alone, thinking things over. Yesterday is history. The rest of your life begins today.

TODAY
I'll have an excellent day.

January 2

"I get really bored if I don't have more
than one thing going on."
Jewel

It's more than boring to do one thing all the
time—whether it's singing, painting, acting, or
playing basketball. It also limits your choices
now and later in life. Washington Redskins
football star Deion Sanders (who doubles as a
professional baseball player) remembers,
"When I was growing up, I gave myself lots of
opportunities to succeed. My thinking? If it
didn't work out in one sport, I wanted to give
myself more chances to be the best in others."

TODAY
I'll try something new.

CONSTRUCTIVE USE OF TIME
ASSET #17: CREATIVE ACTIVITIES

January 3

"It's all right to hold a conversation,
but you should let go of it now and then."
Richard Armour

Think back on the conversations you had today or yesterday—with your family, your friends, in person, on the phone. Who did most of the talking? If the answer is y-o-u, try hard to remember this next time. Back off a bit and let the other person talk. Good conversation is a duet, not a solo act.

TODAY
I'll let other people do some of the talking.

January 4

"Education remains the key to both
economic and political empowerment."
Barbara Jordan

In a study of 20,000 high school teens, nearly
20 percent said they don't try as hard in school
as they could. Why? Because their friends might
think less well of them. 70 percent spend fewer
than five hours a week on homework. Half say
they don't even do the homework that's
assigned. Many believe that "getting by" is
good enough. Minority students may have the
added pressure of being told they're "acting
white" if they achieve in school. Go along with
your friends today, and what happens after
graduation?

TODAY
**I won't let negative peer pressure affect
my school performance.**

January 5

"A school should not be a preparation
for life. A school should be life."
Elbert Hubbard

Your "real life" doesn't start when school ends.
It's happening right now. You spend more time
in school than anywhere else but home. You eat
there, play there, socialize there, learn, laugh,
cry, and probably sleep there on occasion. So
try to find something you like about school—
something you like a lot. Maybe it's a teacher,
maybe it's a class, maybe it's the chance to see
your friends at lunch. Whatever works for you.

TODAY
I'll care about school.

January 6

*"Compassion for our parents
is the true sign of maturity."*
Anaïs Nin

It's not easy being a parent. Just ask one (your own or a friend's). Though parents get to run the show and make the rules, they also have day-to-day responsibilities, problems, and worries, including some you don't have a clue about. Could you hold down a job, manage the house, pay the bills, try to be a decent role model, care for a kid (or two, or more), and still have a life? Imagine what it's like to be your mom or dad. Could your parents use a hug, a kind word, or a little help?

TODAY
I'll go easy on my parents.

SUPPORT
ASSET #1: FAMILY SUPPORT

January 7

"Few things can help an individual more
than to place responsibility on him,
and to let him know that you trust him."
Booker T. Washington

Younger kids love it when older, wiser kids (like you) take them seriously and make them feel wanted and needed. If you're working on a service project, large or small—even if you're just picking up trash on the sidewalk in your neighborhood once a week—invite children you know to help. If you're looking for ways to improve your neighborhood or community, ask children for their ideas and opinions.

TODAY
I'll take a child seriously.

January 8

"I don't know any parents that look
into the eyes of a newborn baby and say,
'How can we screw this kid up?'"
Russell Bishop

On days when your parents say "No, you can't
do that" or "No, you can't go there" or "No,
you can't wear that" or "Just because everyone
else gets to stay out late doesn't mean you can"
or even the dreaded "Because I said so," don't
assume they're trying to ruin your life. Setting
limits is part of their job. Would you rather they
didn't care?

TODAY
**I'll be glad my parents care enough
to set limits for me.**

January 9

"Advice is what we ask for when we already
know the answer but wish we didn't."
Erica Jong

Kings and queens have councillors. Presidents
have cabinets. Corporations have boards. If you
could ask any three adults you know to be your
advisers, who would you choose? You want
people who will be honest with you, even tell
you things you don't really want to hear. Make a
list of possible candidates, but don't stop there.
Talk with at least one of those adults about
something that's been bothering or puzzling you.

TODAY
**I'll talk with an adult
whose opinion I respect.**

January 10

"When prosperity comes,
do not use all of it."
Confucius

Imagine you've just gotten a windfall—a tax refund, or payment for a job you did, or money from your bar/bat mitzvah or birthday or middle-school graduation or Christmas. It's tempting to spend it on something big, like that new bike or stereo you've wanted forever. At least try not to spend every cent. Save some for the future. Put it where it will earn a little interest.

TODAY
I'll spend my money wisely.

January 11

> "Keep away from people who try
> to belittle your ambitions. Small people always
> do that, but the really great make you feel
> that you, too, can become great."
>
> *Mark Twain*

You probably know the kind of "small people" Mark Twain was talking about. They're the ones who say, "Don't try that. It might not work." Or "That's not for you." Or "Don't do that. You're just setting yourself up for disappointment." Or "Forget about it. You'll never do/reach/achieve that." Or "You're not strong enough/smart enough/good enough." Those people are not your friends. Avoid them whenever you can. Find people who will support you, not drag you down.

TODAY
**I'll spend time with someone
who encourages me to do well.**

January 12

"School should be the most beautiful place
in every town and village—so beautiful
that the punishment for undutiful children
should be that they should be barred
from going to school the following day."

Oscar Wilde

Some schools really are beautiful. They stand proudly on city streets or sprawl grandly across acres of manicured lawns. And then there are the schools that don't look so great. If you're stuck in one of the not-so-beautiful schools, you might not be able to do much about years of neglect and underfunding. But you could start a crusade to do what you can. Are there enough trash bins? Do people use them? Can graffiti be cleaned up or painted over?

TODAY
I'll help make my school more appealing.

January 13

> "Dad taught me everything I know.
> Unfortunately, he didn't teach me
> everything he knows."
>
> *Al Unser Jr.*

At some point, usually during our teenage years, we decide that our parents are incredibly stupid. We don't want their advice, there's nothing they can teach us, they don't know anything—that's how we feel. If we're smart, we don't feel that way for long. Because our parents know a lot about quite a few things, and we can save ourselves some time and hurt by learning from them.

TODAY
I'll learn something from my dad or mom.

January 14

"Cherishing children is the mark
of a civilized society."
Joan Ganz Cooney

How do you treat the children you know? Do
you ignore them? Tease them? Barely tolerate
them? To young children, teenagers are heroes.
What a great opportunity for you to help kids
feel valued and appreciated. Smile and say hi
when you see them around. Take a few minutes
to talk with them. Listen to them talk. Laugh at
their jokes. Respect them. They'll feel good
about themselves and even better about you.

TODAY
I'll be nice to the children I know.

January 15

"I totally agree with adults wanting
to step up laws to protect millions of minors."
Brandi, 15

In a nationwide survey of more than 218,000 students in grades 6–12, 50 percent said they support nighttime community curfews for teens. (In a poll of adults, 87 percent favored curfews. No surprises there.) A curfew may cramp your style, but in fact, cities with curfews have fewer juvenile crime victims. Gang violence is down. Residents feel safer. And students are more rested for school. So if your community has a curfew (or your parents have given you one), maybe it's not all bad.

TODAY
**I'll try to see the positive side
of limits like curfews.**

January 16

"We build strong kids, strong families
and strong communities."
YMCA of the USA

When was the last time you stopped by your local Y? It offers much more than hoops, weights, camping, and swimming. Did you know that half of the Y's members nationwide are under 18? Many go for the fun and exercise. Others take advantage of youth programs like the Leaders Clubs, Black Achievers, and YMCA Earth Service Corps. Teens connect with caring adults and get involved in activities that help them grow in positive ways. To find the nearest Y, call 888-333-YMCA or visit the Web site (www.ymca.net).

TODAY
**I'll check into the youth programs
at my local Y.**

January 17

"I was afraid to get up onstage. I thought
I had this horrible voice and I had no control
over it and I felt like an idiot up there."

Liz Phair

Rock singer Liz Phair felt this way *after* her debut album, *Exile in Guyville,* was named Album of the Year by the *Village Voice* and she made the cover of *Rolling Stone.* The point: Even stars can have low self-esteem. Phair hired a vocal coach, joined the 1998 Lilith Fair tour, and learned from other women artists including Natalie Merchant and Sarah McLachlan. Is there something you don't like about yourself? What can you do about it?

TODAY
**I'll do something real to boost
my self-esteem.**

January 18

"Nothing is particularly hard
if you divide it into small jobs."
Henry Ford

Henry Ford invented his Model T, then broke
production down into small jobs with another
innovation: the assembly line. You can take a
similar approach with a big task or project
you're facing. Break it down into steps. Then
plug the steps into your daily planner.
(Assuming you have one—paper, computer, or
Palm. If you don't have a planner, get one. You
can buy a cheap one at a discount store, office
supplies store, or drug store. Or create your
own in a spiral-bound notebook.) Check off the
steps as you do them.

TODAY
**I'll divide a big task or project
into small steps.**

January 19

"A lie comes back sooner or later."
African proverb

You may think a lie is like a balloon, floating harmlessly into the sky and out of your life forever. It's more like a boomerang, circling back to bonk you in the head. Even the littlest fib, the tiniest white lie, the most seemingly harmless untruth can return when you least expect it. Then what? Will you invent another lie, and another? Telling the truth may seem harder at first, when you're on the spot and squirming, but it will save you a lot of time and bother later.

TODAY

I won't lie.

POSITIVE VALUES
ASSET #29: HONESTY

19

January 20

"Learning how to learn is life's most important skill."
Tony Buzan

You're going to forget a lot of what you're learning in school. Hopefully not before the next test, but sooner or later you'll realize that you no longer remember the binomial theorem or who wrote *The Old Man and the Sea*. As long as you know how to learn, you don't have to remember everything. If you think you're not learning how to learn, tell a teacher. Find a tutor. Read a how-to-study guide. Take a class in study skills. Get help. It will make your life easier.

TODAY
I'll work on my study skills.

January 21

"Alone, all alone
Nobody, but nobody
Can make it out here alone."
Maya Angelou

There's no such thing as a self-made man or woman. We all need other people to guide us, encourage us, and help us when we stumble. If you can count on your parents to be there for you, that's great, but it's not enough. You need at least three other adults in your life you can turn to and talk to. Think of adults you know and respect. What about a grandparent? A teacher? A youth leader, counselor, religious leader, or neighbor? A friend's parent?

TODAY
I'll reach out to one adult
I'd like to know better.

SUPPORT
ASSET #3: OTHER ADULT RELATIONSHIPS

January 22

*"If you play it safe in life, you've decided
that you don't want to grow anymore."*
Shirley Hufstedler

When you live in fear, you're less likely to take
positive risks, try new things, and meet new
people. If there's something you're afraid of
that's having a negative impact on your life—if
it's keeping you from having fun, forming relationships, and moving forward—talk with an
adult you trust. Get help facing your fear and
coming up with solutions.

TODAY
I'll face a fear, alone or with help.

January 23

"Sometimes the most important thing in a whole day is the rest we take between two deep breaths, or the turning inwards in prayer for five short minutes."

Etty Hillesum

Prayer can be good for you. Studies suggest that people who pray are less likely to get sick, and people who are prayed for are more likely to get well. Prayer can give you hope, strength, and comfort. It can bring you closer to your God or Higher Power. It can help you resist temptation to do things that conflict with your values. It can guide you to make positive, healthy choices. You might explore the benefits of prayer by talking with your family, friends who share your beliefs, or your religious or spiritual leader.

TODAY
I'll pray or meditate.

CONSTRUCTIVE USE OF TIME
ASSET #19: RELIGIOUS COMMUNITY

January 24

"It is poetry that changes everything."
bell hooks

It may not change everything, but poetry can change a lot of things: the way you feel about the world, your relationships, and yourself, to name a few. Poetry has enormous power to engage our minds and touch our emotions. Try reading some. (Ask a poetry-loving friend or teacher for suggestions.) Try writing some. If you want, you can learn the technical stuff about forms and rhyme and meter. (Take a class or read a book.) Or you can just start writing. Write what's in your heart and on your mind.

TODAY
I'll read or write a poem.

January 25

"Your vision will become clear only
when you can look into your own heart.
Who looks outside, dreams;
who looks inside, awakes."

Carl Jung

Do you believe you're on Earth for a reason?
(Otherwise, what's the point?) Maybe you're
here to make the world a better place. Maybe
you're here to discover, invent, create, or
accomplish something important. Maybe
you're here to be a good person and have some
fun along the way. Give it some thought in your
free time. You might want to jot a few notes in
your journal or planner.

TODAY
I'll look inside.

January 26

"I may not be totally perfect,
but parts of me are excellent."
Ashleigh Brilliant

In a nationwide survey of 272,400 students in grades 6–12, only 31 percent said they were satisfied with their looks. Half of the girls want to lose weight. Half of the boys want to tone up. 85 percent of all teens responding cited ways they'd like to improve. Only 15 percent like themselves "the way I am." And 7 in 10 say they've been depressed. Even if you're feeling down on yourself, there must be *something* you like. Your smile. Your intelligence. Your sense of compassion. Your gift for writing songs or swimming laps or making friends. Or what?

TODABREAK

TODAY

I'll focus on the things I like about myself.

POSITIVE IDENTITY
ASSET #38: SELF-ESTEEM

January 27

"Do not do what you would undo if caught."
Leah Arendt

Fear of getting caught keeps a lot of people honest. There's nothing wrong with that. If your main reason for not pocketing that CD or sneaking into the movie is the worry that someone might see you, that's okay. Rules and laws are supposed to act as deterrents, not just guides to behavior. You don't want to be seen shoplifting. (The shame. The possible call to the police. Your parents. Maybe a fine or worse. Ouch.) It's embarrassing to get kicked out of your local multiplex. Bottom line, it's not worth it.

TODAY
**I'll think about the consequences
of my actions.**

January 28

"Reading is a basic tool
in the living of the good life."
Mortimer Adler

Skating champion Michelle Kwan admits that she didn't read many books when she was growing up. Today she's an avid reader who especially enjoys reading before breakfast. In 1999, she served as chairperson for the American Library Association's Teen Read Week. "I'm here to say reading is cool," she said. "Playing a video game might be fun for five minutes, then it says, 'You're dead. Put another quarter in.'"

TODAY
I'll read.

January 29

*"Keep company with those
who make you better."*
English saying

There are friends who build you up and friends
who drag you down. Friends who support you
and friends who eat away at your self-esteem.
Friends who stand by you and friends who
desert you the minute you make a mistake,
have a problem, or slide down the popularity
scale. Friends you can count on no matter what
and friends who are out for themselves. You're
going to meet and know all kinds of people, but
they won't all be your friends.

TODAY
**I'll spend time with someone
who makes me a better person.**

January 30

"We can tell our values
by looking at our checkbook stubs."
Gloria Steinem

How do you spend your money? Mostly on you? In 1999, Americans between ages 14 and 17 spent $111 *billion*. The average U.S. teen has $94 a week to spend. Multiply that by 52 weeks and get $4,888 a year. That's a lot of clothes, CDs, movies, and fast food. If you have discretionary income (meaning money you can spend however you want), why not give some of it to a worthy cause? Find one that matters to you. Check into it and make sure your money will be put to good use.

TODAY
**I'll support an organization or cause
I care about.**

January 31

"Any man can be a father,
but it takes someone special to be a dad."
Anne Geddes

Which of your parents is most likely to attend a school conference or event? Chances are it's your mom. Here's something interesting to share with your parents: According to a national study, children and teens do better in school when their fathers are involved. Students are more likely to get mostly A's and less likely to repeat a grade. Plus they enjoy school more. This is true whether their fathers live with them or not, and it's true even if their mothers are also involved. In other words, it's best for you if *both* parents are involved in your education.

TODAY
**I'll encourage both of my parents
to be involved in my schooling.**

February 1

"You change into your friends and their actions the more you hang around them."
Posting on a teen message board

If you don't like how your life is going, if you're not comfortable with decisions you're making and directions you're taking, check out your friends. Maybe some of your problems come from trying to fit in and be like them. What else can you do? You can try talking with them. Or you can talk with an adult you trust—someone who will listen and give you good advice. You can find new friends. You might have to be alone for a while, but if you look hard enough and in the right places, you'll meet people who are worth being like.

TODAY
I'll think about whether my friends are helping me or hurting me.

February 2

"Unless what we do is useful,
glory is vain."
Latin proverb

People do crazy things to get attention. Everyone wants to be on TV or in the *Guinness Book of World Records*. If you love the spotlight, try doing something worthwhile to get it. Not that you can't combine crazy with worthwhile. Ryan Tripp was 14 years old when he mowed the lawns at all 50 state capitols and became an official Guinness World Record holder. His real purpose: raising awareness for organ donation.

TODAY
I'll support a cause I care about.

EMPOWERMENT
ASSET #8: YOUTH AS RESOURCES

February 3

"Schools are some of the safest
places in America."
Vincent Schiraldi

A series of school shootings in the 1990s made
it seem like school is a dangerous place to be. In
fact, it's not. Schools are less violent than they
were 10 years ago. Fewer students are carrying
guns or other weapons, and fewer are getting
into fights. Still, it's smart to stay alert and
aware. If you see or hear something that concerns you, resist your natural teenage tendencies
to protect each other and respect privacy. Tell a
teacher.

TODAY
I'll feel safe at school.

SUPPORT
ASSET #5: CARING SCHOOL CLIMATE

February 4

"I know only that what is moral is what you feel good after and what is immoral is what you feel bad after."
Ernest Hemingway

You wake up in the morning after a night out with friends and think, "Ohhhhh noooo, did I really do that?" It's not a pleasant thought. You don't feel good about yourself. Maybe you're embarrassed or even ashamed. Pay attention to those feelings. You can't undo what you did, but you can make better decisions in the future. Just because you did something once doesn't mean you have to do it again. Get help if you need it. Tell an adult you trust. Tell a friend who will stand by you.

TODAY
I'll pay attention to my feelings about what's right and what's wrong.

February 5

*"It is never too late
to give up our prejudices."*
Henry David Thoreau

America is becoming more diverse. In 1860, before the Civil War, there were only three Census categories: white, black, and "quadroon" (someone who was one-quarter black). By 2000, there were 30, from Asian Indian to Other Pacific Islander. Yet in many towns, communities, and cities, race relations are tense. Most hate crimes are racially motivated. And if you think that most are committed by crazed neo-Nazi skinheads, you're wrong. They're committed by otherwise law-abiding young people who are motivated by personal prejudice.

TODAY
I'll examine my prejudices.

February 6

"Change the changeable, accept the unchangeable, and remove yourself from the unacceptable."
Denis Waitley

You may already know the Serenity Prayer: "God, grant me the serenity to accept the things I can't change, courage to change the things I can, and wisdom to know the difference." Motivational speaker Denis Waitley adds another dimension: "Remove yourself from the unacceptable." That's a powerful choice, and you'll probably find that it's based on your personal values. Have you ever walked out of a trashy movie? Or refused to buy a popular CD with violent lyrics? Or turned off the radio rather than listen to a shock jock? If you have, you've made that kind of choice.

TODAY
I'll think deeply about my values.

POSITIVE IDENTITY
ASSET #37: PERSONAL POWER

February 7

"To err is human, but when the eraser
wears out ahead of the pencil,
you're overdoing it."
Josh Jenkins

You rush through your homework so you can
meet your friends or watch your 8:00 TV show.
You race through your report so you can get
back to your video game. Try focusing on
what's in front of you. Ignore distractions.
Don't take phone calls or check your email. Be
purposeful, deliberate, careful. See if it makes a
difference in how you feel about your work—
and how your teacher grades it.

TODAY
I'll take time with my homework.

COMMITMENT TO LEARNING
ASSET #23: HOMEWORK

February 8

> "The biggest mistake is believing there is
> one right way to listen, to talk, to have
> a conversation—or a relationship."
> *Deborah Tannen*

Maybe you don't like how your parents talk to you. Maybe they don't like your attitude. So you all enter each conversation with preconceived ideas about how it's going to go (mainly not well). You might try setting some mutual ground rules. Start with the basics: listen, pay attention, don't interrupt, use respectful words and body language. Agree that you probably have different communication styles. Make a real effort to see each other's point of view. Give a little (compromise) and you might get a lot.

TODAY
I'll watch how I talk to my parents.

February 9

"I'm entirely impressed by the work
that young people are doing,
and I'm extremely angry at many of the people
of my generation…who tend to overlook
the work that young people are doing."
Angela Davis

Angela Davis became politically active in her
early 20s. Maybe that's why she's more aware
than most adults of the positive things young
people today are doing. Too often, grownups
assume that teenagers are slackers, punks, or
juvenile delinquents. If there are adults in your
life who acknowledge your efforts and treat
you with respect, don't take them for granted.
You're lucky and they're rare.

TODAY
**I'll appreciate the adults in my life
who treat me with respect.**

February 10

"Oh how I need
Someone to watch over me."
George and Ira Gershwin

There's one in every neighborhood: The old guy who seems to know everything that's going on. Or the elderly woman who sits by her window all day long, watching. Don't assume they're just nosy or they don't have anything better to do. Maybe the guy reports graffiti he sees in the neighborhood so it gets cleaned up faster. Maybe the woman is the one who called 911 when a fight broke out on your street. Better to be a watcher than someone who pretends not to see.

TODAY
I'll notice what happens in my neighborhood.

February 11

"If anybody wants to keep creating,
they have to be about change."
Miles Davis

Jazz legend Miles Davis was all about change.
He kept evolving throughout his career—trying
new styles, inventing new styles, combining
new rhythms and improvisations, forming and
re-forming the group of musicians he played
with. He recorded over 100 albums, influenced
countless other musicians, and had a powerful
impact on jazz. Who knows what he'd be doing
if he were still around today.

TODAY
**I'll change something I usually do
the same way every day.**

CONSTRUCTIVE USE OF TIME
ASSET #17: CREATIVE ACTIVITIES

February 12

"Nothing external to you
has any power over you."
Ralph Waldo Emerson

You may read Emerson's words and think
"Yeah, right." At this point in your life, it may
seem that everyone and everything has power
over you. Your parents, for starters. Teachers.
Coaches. Other authority figures. Plus all kinds
of rules and laws and restrictions. They may
have power over parts of your life, but they
don't have power over you. You're the boss of
yourself. You're in charge of what you think,
what you believe, and how you feel. You get to
decide the kind of person you are. That's personal power, and it comes from the inside.
Nothing external can change it.

TODAY
I'll know that I have personal power.

POSITIVE IDENTITY
ASSET #37: PERSONAL POWER

February 13

"Whites out of North America!"
Slogan on a T-shirt

That goes for Asians and Hispanics and Africans and Arabs and West Indians and anyone else who wasn't born here or whose ancestors weren't born here. If you're not Native American, get out! Or get smart and celebrate—as in enjoy, explore, value, and delight in—the diversity all around you. In the words of Martin Luther King Jr., "We may have all come on different ships, but we're in the same boat now."

TODAY
I'll be glad I have chances to know different people.

SOCIAL COMPETENCIES
ASSET #34: CULTURAL COMPETENCE

February 14

"To avoid criticism do nothing,
say nothing, be nothing."
Elbert Hubbard

Or risk criticism by acting on, speaking up for, and living by your beliefs. It's a tough choice. No one wants to be criticized. We all want to be accepted and liked. Especially if your beliefs go against the group (your friends, family, or community), being true to yourself can get lonely and kind of scary. Try to surround yourself with people of integrity—friends who walk the walk and talk the talk, even when it's not popular. Then you can support each other.

TODAY
**I'll identify one person I can count on
to stand by me.**

Positive Values
Asset #28: Integrity

February 15

"I not only use all the brains I have,
but all I can borrow."
Woodrow Wilson

If there's something standing between you and success—in school, at work, in your relationships, in your life—you don't have to go it alone. If you've got a problem you just can't solve, you don't have to stay stuck. Unless you live on a desert island, you must know someone you can ask for help. A parent, a teacher, a mentor, a friend, a coach, your school counselor, a youth group leader, a religious leader—who do you trust? Who can you talk to?

TODAY
I'll ask for help if I need it.

COMMITMENT TO LEARNING
ASSET #21: ACHIEVEMENT MOTIVATION

February 16

"The time has come," the Walrus said,
"to talk of many things."
Lewis Carroll

Talk with your parents about school. The good things and the not-so-good things. Your successes, frustrations, irritations, and failures. Funny stories. Sad stories. What you had for lunch and how you think you did on your math test. Why you hate biology (or love it). What you overheard in the hall. The latest rumors. Your hopes and dreams. School is a huge part of your life. Make it part of your parents' life, too.

TODAY
I'll tell my parents what happened in school.

February 17

"Putting off an easy thing makes it hard,
and putting off a hard one makes it impossible."
George H. Lonmer

Some of what people call "being irresponsible" isn't. It's "being forgetful," and it starts with procrastination. You know you're supposed to clean your room, but you're not in the mood, so you put off doing it and suddenly it's the weekend and your dad is yelling, "Why does your room look like a dump?" Not because you disobeyed on purpose. Because you forgot. Hint: You won't forget something if you don't have to remember it. And you won't have to remember if you do it right away. Just get it over with—whether it's a chore, an assignment, a phone call, or a practice session.

TODAY
I'll do something I've been putting off.

POSITIVE VALUES
ASSET #30: RESPONSIBILITY

February 18

"Teens today are exposed to so many more things…. They need adults to set limits and help them make decisions."

Mary Laeger-Hagemeister

It's not that the world was perfect when today's adults were growing up. But your parents and teachers and neighbors weren't exposed to a lot of things you see and hear every day. Movies weren't as violent, music wasn't as explicit, drugs weren't as common, ads weren't as sexy, and guns weren't as easy to get. So when adults set limits for you, maybe they have reasons besides wanting to make your life difficult.

TODAY
**I'll appreciate adults
who are looking out for me.**

February 19

"It takes a village to raise a child."
Benin proverb

"Village" means everyone. Not just parents and other adults. You, too. There are children you probably see every day—on the sidewalk, in the park, in the street, in the elevator. Can you tell them apart? Do you know their names? In their eyes, you're a mighty teenager. You may not notice them, but they notice you. Try reaching out to the kids in your neighborhood. Talk to them. Ask them how they're doing in school. Ask them about their interests—what they like to do for fun. Be a role model and a positive influence in their lives.

TODAY
I'll get to know the children in my neighborhood.

SUPPORT
ASSET #4: CARING NEIGHBORHOOD

February 20

"Teachers open the door,
but you must enter by yourself."
Chinese proverb

If a teacher reaches out to you or offers extra help, say yes. If a coach invites you to join a team, do it if you can. Look around and see what other opportunities are available at your school. Don't graduate wishing you had played basketball, or tried out for the school play, or run for student council, or taken an interesting class, or hung around with a teacher you liked but never got to know.

TODAY
I'll make the most of what my school offers.

February 21

*"A single day is enough to make us
a little larger or, another time, a little smaller."*
Paul Klee

There are days when you feel good about yourself, and days when you feel not so good. What makes the difference? Maybe it has something to do with integrity. Each day you're true to yourself and your values, you get a little stronger. Each time you compromise your values—because you're pressured or weak, lazy or afraid or not paying attention—you lose part of yourself.

TODAY
I'll guard my values carefully.

February 22

"As a class, develop a list
of '100 Things I Like About School.'"
Idea from a school Web site

Try to think of 20 things you like about
school—or 10, or 5. (100 might be pushing it
unless you're super-enthusiastic or you have a
lot of time on your hands.) Here's a sampling of
what other students came up with: "I like having a coach for a teacher." "I like having
English first period so I can get it over with." "I
like my math teacher." "I like being on the
track team." "I like homecoming week." "I like
the media center. There's always a quiet corner
to read in."

TODAY
I'll list some things I like about school.

February 23

"My strength is as the strength of ten
because my heart is pure."
Alfred, Lord Tennyson

When you have a chance, read this quote out loud. You'll feel like a hero—a knight in shining armor, or Joan of Arc. What does it mean to have a pure heart? You may have your own ideas about that. If you don't, try some of these: To be faithful and true to yourself. To know what your values are and live by them, even when it's not easy. To resist temptation and pressure. To feel good about who you are, what you stand for, and what you believe in. To hold your head high.

TODAY

I'll be strong.

POSITIVE IDENTITY
ASSET #37: PERSONAL POWER

February 24

> "Individual commitment to a group effort—
> that is what makes a team work, a company
> work, a society work, a civilization work."
> *Vince Lombardi*

You're thinking about joining a youth program, but you're not sure what's in it for you. Of course, that depends on the program, but here's a general idea of what most have to offer: A safe place to go. Fun and meaningful things to do. Opportunities to build relationships with caring adults. Chances to meet new people and make new friends. Lots of occasions to see positive role models in action. Time to learn positive values and think about your own values. Ways to build your self-esteem. And that's just for starters.

TODAY

I'll check out the youth programs in my area.

February 25

"Life is full of responsibility
and tough decisions. Why take on more
than you can handle?"
Christy, 17

Feeling pressured to do something you know you shouldn't? Something risky or dangerous or just plain dumb? Not sure how to back out and save face? Try saying "No, thanks. My parents would kill me." Use Mom and Dad as your excuse. Even if you've never talked with them about the situation you're in (and especially if you have), go ahead and blame your decision on them. If they knew, they wouldn't mind.

TODAY
**I'll be guided by my parents'
good wishes for me.**

BOUNDARIES AND EXPECTATIONS
ASSET #11: FAMILY BOUNDARIES

February 26

"I got a simple rule about everybody.
If you don't treat me right—shame on you!"
Louis Armstrong

Do other people get on your case? Tell you to
be like this person or that person, less one way
and more another? Imply that you're just not
good enough? Say that you'll never amount to
much if you don't aim for a particular goal or
meet a particular expectation (usually theirs),
that you won't get anywhere because you're not
smart enough or attractive enough or motivated enough? Their opinion is not your problem.
It's their problem. And if they think put-downs
do any good, it's not their only problem.

TODAY
**I won't let anyone else determine
how I feel about myself.**

February 27

"In high school, I spent most of my time hanging out with my mom, going shopping and talking for hours. To this day, my mom is one of my best friends."
Liv Tyler

Are your parents just your parents, or are they also your friends? If they're not your friends yet, can you see the potential? One bonus of growing up is the chance to build a different kind of relationship with Mom and Dad. They'll always be your parents, probably a little too eager to give you advice, but as you all get older and wiser, the way you relate to each other will change. You might even become close friends. Why not? You probably have some things in common already—shared interests, shared values, and maybe a passion for Grandma's lasagna.

TODAY
I'll hang out with my parents.

SUPPORT
ASSET #1: FAMILY SUPPORT

February 28

"Don't be embarrassed by your
achievements.... Never lower your standards."
Martha Stewart

If there's something you're really good at, go
for it. If your friends give you a hard time
because you ace the math tests or star in the
school plays or hit the home runs or win the
writing contests, don't let them stop you or
slow you down. Before too long, you'll be on
your own and their opinions won't matter. Try
to find people who will support and encourage
you, even if this means making new friends.

TODAY
I'll be proud of my achievements.

February 29

"We make a living by what we get;
we make a life by what we give."
Winston Churchill

You can spend your life getting, and what do you have in the end? Things. Or you can give your time and energy, sweat and muscle, smarts and heart, and you might change another life (or many lives) for the better. What can you give right now? Who needs it? Ask around your family, school, neighborhood, or faith community. Maybe a friend could use someone to listen. That's giving, too.

TODAY
I'll give.

POSITIVE VALUES
ASSET #26: CARING

March 1

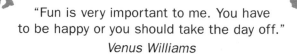

"Fun is very important to me. You have
to be happy or you should take the day off."
Venus Williams

Tennis champion Venus Williams is a model of
confidence, optimism, and achievement. She
also seems to love her life—playing, winning,
traveling the world. In almost every photo-
graph you see of her, unless she's slamming the
ball, she's all smiles. Even if you're not one of
the world's greatest athletes, you have something in common with Venus: You have the
power to be happy with your life.

TODAY
I'll be happy.

POSITIVE IDENTITY
ASSET #37: PERSONAL POWER

March 2

"Since it doesn't cost a dime to dream,
you'll never shortchange yourself
when you stretch your imagination."
Robert Schuller

Your imagination is where ideas happen. Creativity lives there. And inventiveness. Inspiration, too. Sometimes problems go there to be solved. Even if you're overscheduled, overcommitted, and overwhelmed, try to spend some time each day stretching your imagination. Think wild and crazy thoughts. Visualize pictures in your mind. Hear music. See what pops up, floats in, and drifts out. It's fun, it's entertaining, and it's free.

TODAY
I'll dream.

March 3

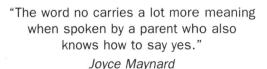

"The word no carries a lot more meaning
when spoken by a parent who also
knows how to say yes."
Joyce Maynard

If all your parents ever say is no (or that's how
it seems to you), try talking with them. Explain
that you need more freedom and ask how you
can earn it. Be polite and respectful. Listen to
their opinions and concerns. Remind them that
you won't be living at home forever (parents
sometimes seem to forget this), and you need
practice now making choices and decisions on
your own. See if they're willing to loosen their
grip a little.

TODAY
I'll talk with my parents about limits.

March 4

"We need to make sure that no boy or girl
in America is growing up without having
in his or her life the presence
of a responsible, caring adult."

General Colin L. Powell

As Chairman of the Joint Chiefs of Staff,
General Colin Powell advised three U.S. presidents. Currently he chairs America's Promise:
The Alliance for Youth, a national crusade
aimed at building and strengthening the character and competence of children and young
people. To learn what America's Promise is
doing for kids in your community, visit the Web
site (www.americaspromise.org).

TODAY
**I'll learn about America's Promise
or another program that helps
kids and teens in my community.**

EMPOWERMENT
ASSET #7: COMMUNITY VALUES YOUTH

March 5

"The love and support I get from my family
goes a long way, and helps me get through
the hardest times.... For me,
family is everything."
Monica

No family is perfect. All families have problems. Some families are seriously messed up. If you feel loved and supported in your family—if you know they're there for you no matter what—you're beyond lucky. You're blessed. Think of the hard times you've gone through. Think of how much harder those times would have been if you were on your own. If you don't feel loved and supported at home, think of other people who care about you.

TODAY
I'll be grateful for my family.

March 6

"Develop a passion for learning.
If you do, you will never cease to grow."
Anthony J. D'Angelo

Some people need a reason to learn something
new. If they can't see how it will help them
reach a specific goal (passing a test, meeting a
requirement, improving a grade), they're not
interested. They turn learning into a chore and
a bore. If you can, avoid that trap. Try to enjoy
learning for its own sake—because it's there,
because you can do it, because it feels good, because
it's fun to have a head full of interesting things.

TODAY

I'll learn something for the fun of it.

COMMITMENT TO LEARNING
ASSET #22: SCHOOL ENGAGEMENT

March 7

"Both tears and sweat are salty, but they render a different result. Tears will get you sympathy, sweat will get you change."

Jesse Jackson

Sometimes it seems like the world is unbearably sad and cruel. People are starving, homeless, unjustly imprisoned, suffering from one disaster or another, forced to become refugees...the list of human tragedies goes on and on. Sometimes a story you see or read might make you cry. Crying is good; it shows that you have compassion. But it's not enough. By helping other people, you can relieve some of the suffering in the world. Every caring act matters, no matter how small or insignificant it may seem.

TODAY

I'll perform a caring act—something specific that helps at least one other person.

March 8

> "The measure of success is not whether
> you have a tough problem to deal with, but
> whether it's the same problem you had last year."
> *John Foster Dulles*

If you're still arguing with your parents about curfew, still turning your homework in late, still forgetting your locker combination, still spending too much time surfing the Web, why not do something about it? Most problems are solvable if you take the time, make the effort, and plan your approach. Procrastination is an energy drain. If you have a problem that's been hanging around too long, maybe it's time to fix it, get help, or just let it go.

TODAY
I'll try to resolve an old problem.

Social Competencies
Asset #32: Planning and Decision Making

March 9

"Regret has no cure, but it can
easily be prevented."
Ralph Marston

Words you didn't say. Things you didn't do.
Places you didn't go. People you didn't get to
know. Do you have a long personal list of
would haves, could haves, should haves (and
shouldn't haves)? What a burden. You've got
the power to live without regret, starting today.
Take advantage of opportunities that are given
to you. Make your own opportunities. Act positively and don't delay. Then tomorrow, a year
from now, five years from now, you can say
"I'm glad I did that" instead of "I'm sorry I
didn't."

TODAY
I'll live fully—no regrets.

March 10

"I loved school!"
Kevin Richardson

In case you've just arrived from another planet and don't know this yet, Kevin Richardson is a member of the Backstreet Boys, one of the biggest pop groups in the world. He and his cousin Brian Littrell (another BSB) grew up and went to school in Lexington, Kentucky. Brian received his first set of keyboards as a high school freshman and spent his teen years in chorus and drama club. He remembers having "a great childhood"—part of which involved loving school.

TODAY
I'll have a positive attitude toward school.

COMMITMENT TO LEARNING
ASSET #24: BONDING TO SCHOOL

March 11

*"If at first the idea is not absurd,
then there is no hope for it."*
Albert Einstein

People all over the world are desperate for safe,
decent, affordable shelter. What about building
houses with the people who need them, working side-by-side, then selling the homes at no
profit and without charging any interest on the
mortgage? It's a crazy idea, it'll never
work...and it's called Habitat for Humanity,
which has built more than 95,000 houses in 60
countries since 1976. Maybe you've got a plan
for helping people and reducing world poverty
and hunger.

TODAY

I'll have a crazy idea for changing the world.

March 12

> "It is the mark of an educated mind
> to be able to entertain a thought
> without accepting it."
>
> *Aristotle*

Some people you know—including your friends—will try to talk you into doing things you don't want to do, know you shouldn't do, or aren't sure about. Go ahead and listen to their arguments and persuasions. Then ask them to return the favor by listening to you. Explain why you've decided not to go along with them. Be clear about your reasons. Maybe what they want to do is against your personal values or beliefs. Maybe you think it's an unsafe risk. Your willingness to listen may give you the chance to have a positive influence on others.

TODAY
**I'll keep communication open
even when I don't agree.**

SOCIAL COMPETENCIES
ASSET #35: RESISTANCE SKILLS

March 13

"Good communication is stimulating
as black coffee, and just as hard
to sleep after."
Anne Morrow Lindbergh

When's the last time you had a really great conversation with your parents? Maybe you sat around the breakfast table on Sunday morning until the leftover eggs on your plate turned to stone. Or maybe you talked in the car on the way home from a game, then sat in the driveway in the dark, still talking. The older you get, the more interesting conversations with your parents can become. If you haven't formed the family habit of good communication, it's not too late. You start.

TODAY
I'll talk to my parents.

March 14

"Ask not what your country can do for you.
Ask what you can do for your country."
President John F. Kennedy

Maybe you live in a community that doesn't do much for kids and teens. You can sit around wishing there were places to go and things to do, or you can take an active role. Get together with friends who feel the way you do and make a plan. Write letters to the editor of your local newspaper. Meet with community groups— Rotary, Kiwanis, or Lions clubs, veterans' organizations, and anyone else who will listen—and ask for their help. Is there a building downtown that's not being used? A church or synagogue that's willing to turn a room into a teen center?

TODAY
I'll do something for my community.

EMPOWERMENT
ASSET #8: YOUTH AS RESOURCES

March 15

"There are no exceptions to the rule
that everybody likes to be
an exception to the rule."
Charles Osgood

If you go to a school with a lot of rules, it can
get annoying. Maybe there's a no-piercings
rule, and you feel that a pierced eyebrow is the
only way to express yourself personally and
aesthetically. Or maybe you're not allowed to
wear anything that might be mistaken for a
gang symbol. Or maybe you can't wear your
favorite T-shirt because it's offensive to some
people. Before you decide to fight a rule all the
way to the top, think about whether you'll even
care in a month or a year or five years from
now. Is it really that important?

TODAY

I'll choose my battles carefully.

March 16

"It's great to reach out and help."
Gregory Hines

Actor and dancer Gregory Hines is talking about mentoring. He recently took part in a national program that linked kids across America with prominent mentors, from astronaut Andrew Allen to musician "Babyface" Edmonds, track star Jackie Joyner-Kersee, Minnesota governor Jesse Ventura, and video director Billie Woodruff, to name just a few. When you find a mentor or join a youth program, you'll connect with adults who are there for you because they want to be. Most are unpaid volunteers. All have a sincere interest in youth. Mentoring programs and youth programs are great opportunities for you. What are you waiting for?

TODAY

I'll find a mentor or join a youth program.

March 17

"Hold your head high, stick your chest out.
You can make it. It gets dark sometimes
but morning comes.... Keep hope alive."
Jesse Jackson

Viktor Frankl could easily have lost all hope.
During World War II, he was held in the Nazi
concentration camp at Auschwitz for three
years. His father, mother, brother, and wife all
died in the camps. Yet Frankl stayed optimistic
about his future. In *Man's Search for Meaning*,
he wrote, "Everything can be taken from a man
but one thing: the last of human freedoms—to
choose one's own attitude in any given set of cir-
cumstances." If Frankl could believe this despite
the horrors he experienced, what about you?

TODAY
I'll choose to have a positive attitude.

March 18

"You're either part of the solution
or part of the problem."
Eldridge Cleaver

Chances are, you already know many people of mixed backgrounds and different cultures. If you don't, what's stopping you? Bias? Prejudice? Fear? Laziness? Lack of opportunities? You're marooned on a desert island? Or what? There's really no excuse for living in a narrow world. If you're held back by bias, prejudice, or fear, talk with adults you trust. Talk with friends you respect. Don't limit yourself any longer.

TODAY
**I'll make an effort to broaden
my circle of friends.**

March 19

"My family gave me values
that have sustained me through situations
that would challenge any person."
Kathy Ireland

Thanks to politics, family values have gotten a
bad reputation. Some people think they mean
"my family is better than yours" or "if you
don't believe what we do and act like we do,
you're wrong." In fact, all families have values:
ideals, beliefs, and standards that are important to them. You might talk with your family
about your family values. Do you believe in
caring? Honesty? Kindness? Keeping promises?
Respect? Responsibility?

TODAY
I'll explore my family's values.

March 20

"Commitment leads to action.
Action brings your dream closer."
Marcia Wieder

You dream about finishing your homework
early, of having free time to do what you want.
You chew your pencil, surf the Web, grab a
snack, pet the dog, call a friend, watch a little
MTV, doodle, check your email, and guess
what, an hour has gone by and you're still
dreaming about finishing your homework early.
Too late. Maybe tomorrow…. Or maybe today
you can promise yourself, "I'll start my homework right away and stick with it until I'm
done."

TODAY
**I'll commit to doing my homework
without distractions or procrastinating.**

COMMITMENT TO LEARNING
ASSET #23: HOMEWORK

March 21

"The first three years of school
were wonderful. After that, it was the abyss
until I got into high school,
where it became wonderful again."
Madeleine L'Engle

Nobody loves every minute of their school experience. Even adults who say they loved school can probably remember at least one year (maybe more) when they didn't. You'll have classes you don't like and teachers you can't stand. And you'll get over it. Besides, school is much more than classes and teachers. It's friends and sports and social activities. Focus on those when other things aren't so good.

TODAY
I'll know that school has ups and downs.

COMMITMENT TO LEARNING
ASSET #24: BONDING TO SCHOOL

March 22

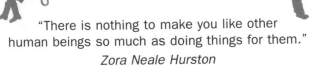

"There is nothing to make you like other human beings so much as doing things for them."
Zora Neale Hurston

Teens and young adults are volunteering in record numbers. A 1997 survey showed that 73 percent of 15- to 29-year-olds had volunteered or worked for a community organization at some point during their lives. If you're looking for ways to help, check out National Youth Service Day, the largest service event in the world. It falls on the third Tuesday of April, so you've got time to plan ahead. For more information, call Youth Service America, (202) 296-2992. Or visit the Servenet Web site (www.servenet.org) and click on the National Youth Service Day icon.

TODAY
I'll make a commitment to serve.

EMPOWERMENT
ASSET #9: SERVICE TO OTHERS

March 23

"A good neighbor is a fellow who smiles at you over the back fence, but doesn't climb over it."

Bugs Baer

Maybe you think your neighbors should mind their own business. Maybe you're mad because the person next door told your parents about the party you had when they were out of town. Or you wish the people across the hall would stop nagging you for playing your music too loud. On the other hand, you could be glad that people notice you at all.

TODAY
I'll be more respectful of my neighbors.

March 24

"I learned things that were to change my life forever."

Al, 16

Al is talking about his experiences in Young Life, a Christian ministry that reaches out to junior high and high school kids. Weekly meetings and summer camps bring kids together with peers and adult leaders to explore their faith, build relationships, and have fun. Young Life (www.younglife.org) is one of many national religious organizations for youth. Another is B'nai B'rith Youth Organization (www.bnaibrith.org). If you'd like to find an organization that fits your beliefs, talk with a parent, youth leader, or spiritual leader.

TODAY

I'll look into religious organizations for kids and teens in my community.

March 25

> "If you never change your mind,
> why have one?"
> *Edward De Bono*

A leading feminist and founder of *Ms.* magazine, Gloria Steinem once believed that marriage destroys relationships. In 1987, she said, "I don't think marriage has a good name.... Legally speaking, it was designed for a person and a half. You became a semi-non-person when you got married." In September 2000, at age 66, she got married. You may think you'll feel the same about certain things for the rest of your life, but you won't. The more you experience, the more you learn, the more choices you make, the more you'll change. You always have the power to change your mind.

TODAY

I'll keep an open mind.

March 26

"Everyone has a 'risk muscle.'
You keep it in shape by trying new things.
If you don't, it atrophies. Make a point
of using it at least once a day."

Roger von Oech

Do you take learning risks, or do you learn only what you have to? You might try a class at school that interests you, even if you don't need it to graduate or get into college. Outside of school, explore libraries, museums, community ed classes, and local colleges. Read a book on a subject you know nothing about. Rent a foreign film on video or DVD. Explore a Web site on a topic that's new to you. Listen to music that's completely different from what you usually like. Exercise your risk muscle and your mental muscles at the same time.

TODAY
I'll take a learning risk.

COMMITMENT TO LEARNING
ASSET #22: SCHOOL ENGAGEMENT

March 27

"Truth is not determined by majority vote."
Doug Gwyn

You're with a group of friends at the mall when you find somebody's wallet. There's money in it, plus ID and credit cards. Your friends all think you should keep the money and split it with them. Then you can drop the wallet in the Lost and Found and no one will ever know. Besides, the owner cares most about the ID and cards, right? What will you do? P.S. An online poll asked, "If you found a wallet, would you return it?" 73 percent of the respondents said "yes." 18 percent said "yes, but I'd keep the money." 9 percent said "no."

TODAY

I'll do the right thing.

March 28

"Homework happens."
Trevor Romain

Homework is a fact of life as long as you're in school. You can't escape it. You can't avoid it. You can't wish it away. You can, if you want, try to have a more positive attitude about homework, which will make doing it a bit more bearable. Here are three good reasons to do your homework: 1) It strengthens skills you need to succeed in school and in life. 2) It makes you smarter. (Not always, but sometimes you actually learn something from doing your homework.) 3) It teaches responsibility.

TODAY
I won't complain about homework.

COMMITMENT TO LEARNING
ASSET #23: HOMEWORK

March 29

"It's not what you know,
but who you know."
Anonymous

Networking. The dictionary defines it as "the exchange of information or services among individuals, groups, or institutions." You're not too young to start networking. Are there adults you know and admire? What about neighbors? Friends of your parents? Parents of your friends? If they know you, and you feel they have a good opinion of you, consider asking them for a job reference or letter of recommendation. Then, if you get the job, be sure to tell them and say thanks for their help. Get back in touch every now and then to let them know how you're doing. You might start a relationship that will last for years.

TODAY
I'll do some networking.

SUPPORT
ASSET #3: OTHER ADULT RELATIONSHIPS

March 30

"Do not stand in a place of danger
trusting in miracles."
Arabian proverb

If there's someplace that feels unsafe to you,
don't go there. Even if your friends do. Even if
they pressure you or make fun of you for not
going. If it means taking the long way around a
certain park in your neighborhood or hallway
in your school, protect yourself. You're not
being a coward. You're being smart.

TODAY

I'll avoid places where I don't feel safe.

EMPOWERMENT
ASSET #10: SAFETY

March 31

"Tiger Woods is a great golfer,
but he is a much better person."
Earl Woods

The youngest player ever to win golf's Grand
Slam, Tiger Woods knows he's a role model. He
wants to be, and he takes his responsibilities
very seriously. The Tiger Woods Foundation,
which Tiger established with his father, Earl,
supports programs across the U.S. that help
kids and families. As part of the Foundation's
activities, Tiger travels around the country giving personal golf lessons—and inspiration—to
kids at his Junior Golf Clinics. He has said, "I
am committed to giving the best of myself."

TODAY
**I'll identify at least one person
who's a role model for me.**

April 1

"Drinking does not make you mature,
cool or popular no matter what you think."
Posting on a teen message board

April is Alcohol Awareness Month. It's a good
time to learn the facts about what drinking can
do to you. Fact #1: Alcohol goes directly into
the bloodstream and affects every system in the
body. Fact #2: Alcohol lowers inhibitions and
impairs judgment, which can lead to risky
behaviors. Fact #3: Alcohol hinders coordina-
tion, slows reaction time, dulls senses, and
blocks memory functions. Fact #4: Alcohol can
give you bad breath and hangovers and has lots
of calories. Fact #5: Every three hours, a
teenager dies in an alcohol-related car crash.
Want to know more? Check out the Prevention
Online Web site (www.health.org).

TODAY
I won't use alcohol.

POSITIVE VALUES
ASSET #31: RESTRAINT

April 2

"Violence is not just an inner-city problem.
Violence is America's problem."
Linda Lantieri

Linda Lantieri is founding director of the Resolving Conflict Creatively Program, which has taught thousands of students and teachers how to respond nonviolently to conflict. Research has shown that conflict resolution programs like RCCP work. Your school should offer some kind of conflict resolution, violence prevention, or peer mediation program—or all three. If it doesn't, talk with your parents, teachers, and principal. Meanwhile, you can learn more about RCCP at the Web site (www.esrnational.org).

TODAY
**I'll advocate for conflict resolution
education in my school.**

April 3

"My only advice is to stay aware, listen
carefully, and yell for help if you need it."
Judy Blume

In trouble? Need help? Dial P-A-R-E-N-T-S.
Okay, not really—you'll get a wrong number.
But see if your parents will make an agreement
with you. Your side: If you ever find yourself in
a risky situation and you need a way out, you'll
call them. Their side: If you call them, they'll
come and get you—from any place, at any time,
with no questions asked. Because the last part
will drive your parents crazy, you also have to
agree to tell them what happened the next day
(or soon after), when you're all able to talk
calmly.

TODAY
I'll make an agreement with my parents.

POSITIVE VALUES
ASSET #31: RESTRAINT

April 4

"If you wish to be a good reader, read."
Epictetus

Reading for pleasure—just because you want to, not because you have to—makes you a better reader. Reading something challenging builds your reading skills even more. Try a hard book on a topic you know a lot about. Or a not-so-hard book on a topic that's new to you. Or a book that's won a prestigious award— a Pulitzer or Nobel or National Book Award or Hugo (science fiction) or Edgar (mystery) or Booker Prize (England's top literary award). Need suggestions? Ask a librarian, a media center specialist, or a passionate reader you know.

TODAY
I'll read something challenging.

April 5

"We care enough to come out
to where they are."
Larry Lucio

Larry Lucio is principal of a Minneapolis,
Minnesota, high school. One August, just
before school started for the fall, he and a team
of staff members went door-to-door, greeting
students' parents, handing out fliers with
school phone numbers and information, and
inviting parents to attend freshman orientation.
Their goal: to get parents involved in their kids'
schooling. Most parents they met were pleas-
antly surprised, and one even asked the team to
stay for dinner. Sometimes all parents need is an
invitation.

TODAY
I'll invite my parents to a school event.

SUPPORT
ASSET #6: PARENT INVOLVEMENT IN SCHOOLING

April 6

"My fears and insecurities have passed
now, with the help of a warm
and understanding family."
Melissa Esposito

Many parents think they talk to their kids
about important issues, but kids don't always
agree. In a recent poll, 8 in 10 parents said they
had talked with their kids about ways to protect themselves from violence, but only 6 in 10
kids remembered having such conversations. If
you want your parents' advice on how to stay
safe—or any other topic that concerns you—
ask. If you don't get what you need from them,
talk with another adult you trust.

TODAY
**I'll talk with my parents
about ways to stay safe.**

April 7

"You can't base your life
on other people's expectations."
Stevie Wonder

If there are people who expect good things of
you, be glad. You need their encouragement
and support, their advice and insights, and (in
the future, when you're college-hunting or job-
hunting), their recommendations and connections. But the only person you really need to
satisfy is you. Do you know what you want
from life? Some people write their hopes and
dreams in a journal. They check back from
time to time to see if they're on track. They add
new hopes and dreams and modify old ones.
You might try this and see if it works for you.

TODAY
**I'll write down my expectations for
myself—my personal hopes and dreams.**

BOUNDARIES AND EXPECTATIONS
ASSET #16: HIGH EXPECTATIONS

April 8

"A home is not a mere transient shelter.
Its essence lies in the personalities
of the people who live in it."

H.L. Mencken

Think of three things you like about your mom.
Your dad. Your sister(s) or brother(s). Other
family members you live with (grandparents,
aunts, uncles, stepparents, etc.). Was that hard?
Now think of at least one thing that makes
each person in your family unique. For your
mom, is it her goofy laugh? Or the fact that she
reads more books than any other mother you
know? Does your dad know way too much
about the Beatles? Does your grandma always
win at poker?

TODAY

I'll appreciate my family.

April 9

"Fear less, hope more, eat less,
chew more, whine less, breathe more,
talk less, say more, hate less, love more,
and all good things will be yours."

Swedish proverb

If only it were that simple. Hmmm...maybe it is. When you fear less, you take more risks. When you hope more, you have a positive attitude toward life. When you whine less, people like you more. Breathing (from your diaphragm, not your chest) is a proven stress-reliever. When you talk less, you can listen more. When you hate less, you're not angry all the time. When you love more, you're more lovable. You might want to write this saying in your journal or notebook. It's good advice.

TODAY
**I'll choose one good thing to do more,
one not-so-good thing to do less.**

April 10

> "No trumpets sound when the
> important decisions of our life are made.
> Destiny is made known silently."
>
> *Agnes DeMille*

You've already made some decisions that are shaping your future. Maybe you've talked them over with people you're close to. Maybe you're keeping them private for now because you think other people won't understand. Perhaps you've looked around at your family and friends and told yourself, "I don't want to be like them. I want to be different." You might make a list of important decisions you've made. Put it where no one else will find it, and refer to it when you need reinforcement.

TODAY
I'll follow my own path.

SOCIAL COMPETENCIES
ASSET #35: RESISTANCE SKILLS

April 11

"If I am not for myself, who will be for me?
If I am not for others, what am I?
And if not now, when?"
Rabbi Hillel

Are you a caring person? Are you someone who has empathy for others? Who treats other people with kindness and respect? Who looks for ways to help others? Are you someone who serves? Who speaks out for people who can't speak for themselves? Who donates time, energy, effort, and money to worthy causes? If you aren't, why not? If you're waiting, what for?

TODAY
I'll care.

POSITIVE VALUES
ASSET #26: CARING

April 12

"The only way you can make good
at anything is to practice,
and then practice some more."
Pete Rose

Homework is practice—in solving problems,
finding answers, getting organized, planning,
writing, spelling, and other skills that come in
handy throughout life. Even dull, boring homework is a type of practice, like playing scales on
the piano or shooting baskets at the park. If all
or most of your homework is dull and boring,
talk with your teachers and see if there are
other options available. Maybe they can give
you assignments that are more interesting and
meaningful for you.

TODAY
I'll focus on the benefits of doing homework.

April 13

"Hope is a gift we give ourselves."
Naomi Judd

As you visualize your future—who, where, and what you'll be—try to have hope. Hope is a leap of faith. Hope is optimism, confidence, the belief that things will turn out okay no matter what. If you form the habit of hopefulness, if you start and end each day being hopeful, you'll get through even the hardest times, because you'll know that things will get better. Poet Emily Dickinson described hope as "the thing with feathers/that perches in the soul/and sings the tune without the words/and never stops at all…." Can you hear it?

TODAY

I'll be hopeful.

POSITIVE IDENTITY
ASSET #40: POSITIVE VIEW OF PERSONAL FUTURE

April 14

"To achieve the impossible dream,
try going to sleep."
Joan Klempner

Running around all the time? Too busy? Overcommitted? Feeling tired? Finding it hard to meet your goals? Go home and get some sleep. Almost 100 million American adults have sleep problems that affect their performance at work. If you're nodding off in third hour, you may be sleep-deprived. When you don't get enough sleep, you build up a "sleep debt." Try going to bed a little earlier and getting up at the same time every morning. You'll have more mental energy for school and fun.

TODAY
I'll get enough sleep.

CONSTRUCTIVE USE OF TIME
ASSET #20: TIME AT HOME

April 15

"Why are all our heroes so imperfect?"
Jill Sobule

If you think your role models should be perfect,
you're doomed. Everyone makes mistakes.
Everyone stumbles. Everyone screws up.
Nobody does the right thing all the time. The
difference is, role models work to overcome
their flaws and learn from their mistakes. What
if you learn that someone you admire did something really stupid 10 years ago? Before you pass
judgment, look at what the person has done in
the 10 years since then. People can change.

TODAY
**I'll know that role models
don't have to be perfect.**

BOUNDARIES AND EXPECTATIONS
ASSET #14: ADULT ROLE MODELS

April 16

*"Violence in our schools is
not acceptable, not at all, not ever."*
Louis J. Freeh

What is your school doing to prevent violence?
Does it have and enforce a zero-tolerance policy toward weapons, violence, harassment, and
racial incidents? At one Virginia high school
with a zero-tolerance policy toward guns and
drugs, suspensions are down 40 percent since
the policy took effect. These policies aren't
always perfect, but they do discourage behaviors that can lead to trouble.

TODAY
**I'll support a zero-tolerance policy
at my school.**

April 17

*"The real art of conversation is not only
to say the right thing in the right place,
but, far more difficult still, to leave unsaid
the wrong thing at the tempting moment."*
Dorothy Nevill

What's good about being a family is you can
say anything to each other. What's bad about
being a family is sometimes you do. In
moments of frustration, anger, or rage, we say
things to our parents that we would never say
to our worst enemies. If you've ever wanted to
take back something you've said—if you've
seen that look of pain in your parents' eyes and
wished you could eat your words—that's a sign
of compassion and maturity.

TODAY

I'll think before I speak.

SUPPORT
ASSET #2: POSITIVE FAMILY COMMUNICATION

April 18

> "Take a look at those two open hands
> of yours. They are tools with which to serve,
> make friends, and reach out for the best in life."
> *Wilfred A. Peterson*

Here's how to bond with your school: Help it. An Alabama high-school student thought his small rural school should have computers. Today it does, thanks to his efforts—initiating fundraisers, getting grants, arranging for donations, installing software, training younger students so the project could continue after he graduated. An Iowa middle-school student volunteered 10 hours each week to help his school janitorial staff clean the school. What can you do?

TODAY
I'll serve my school.

April 19

"Be just, and fear not."
William Shakespeare

Could you walk up to a homeless person on the street and hand him a blanket and pillow? Trevor Ferrell did when he was 11 years old. By the time Trevor was 16, he and his family had opened a homeless shelter in downtown Philadelphia, Pennsylvania, called Trevor's Place. That was followed by Trevor's Next Door, a center for women and children. At the time of this writing, Trevor is trying to start a Youth Farm School for inner-city kids. You might look him up on the Web, see how he's doing, and learn how you can help. (Use a search engine to find him.)

TODON

TODAY
I'll reach out to a person in need.

April 20

"Among my most prized possessions
are words that I have never spoken."
Orson Scott Card

You used to get shoved on the playground for
calling people names. Now you might get shot
in the street. Careless words, angry words,
offensive words, and words perceived as disre-
spectful can and do spark violence. Be careful
what you say. Think before you speak. Stay out
of dissing contests. Let insults roll off you.
Walk away.

TODAY
I'll avoid verbal confrontations.

April 21

"Sports...develop integrity, self-reliance and initiative. They teach you a lot about working in groups."
Byron R. White

Maybe you thought sports were mostly about sweat and pain and screaming coaches. Guess again. Sports build skills, smarts, and self-confidence that will help you succeed in all areas of your life, starting now and continuing through your adult years and careers. If you're not part of a team, think about joining one. If school teams aren't for you, look around your town or city. What about community centers? Gyms? The YMCA or YWCA? A league at your local bowling alley?

TODAY

I'll learn about sports available to me in my school and community.

April 22

"It is the mind that makes the body."
Sojourner Truth

When you look in the mirror, what do you see? Someone who's too fat or too thin? Maybe your body image is all in your head. Especially when there's so much pressure to be perfect (thanks to movies, magazines, TV, and advertising), teens everywhere are feeling as if they don't measure up. Are you healthy and fit? Do you eat sensibly (usually) and exercise (often enough)? Stop beating yourself up for not looking like a supermodel. Just for today, accept yourself the way you are.

TODAY
I'll be happy in my body.

April 23

"Violence is the last refuge
of the incompetent."
Salvor Hardin

There is always an alternative to violence. It
takes time and thought, preparation, patience,
and a willingness to listen, look for solutions,
compromise, and try again. Talk about small
conflicts before they become big problems. If
you're angry, talk more quietly than usual. The
other person will have to listen more carefully
to hear you and may lower his or her voice, too.
Instead of shouting at each other, you can have
a real conversation.

TODAY
**I'll take a personal vow
to resolve conflicts nonviolently.**

April 24

"There is no good reason why
we should not develop and change
until the last day we live."
Karen Horney

You're a work in progress. You'll still be a
work in progress when you're 30 or 60 or 90
or 110 years old. (Scientists today are saying
that prevention and elimination of disease,
along with control over the aging process,
could push human life spans that far.) One key
to living an interesting, satisfying life is learning. You're in school now because you have to
be, but what about later? Are you a reader? Do
you enjoy learning new things? Can you see
yourself developing new interests and passions
at every stage of your life?

TODAY
**I'll make a personal commitment
to be a lifelong learner.**

April 25

"If you get lost in a book, everything that's bothering you just goes away."
Brandon Keefe

Reading can be a great escape. When you're sad or mad, frustrated or lonely, reach for a book and let it carry you to another time and place. Find one that grabs you from the very first page. If you're not sure what's good, ask a librarian or a friend who loves to read. P.S. California teen Brandon Keefe is more than an eager reader. He also collects books for needy schools and communities through Bookends, a nonprofit organization he helped to start. If you buy the books you read, consider donating them to a school or children's home when you're through with them.

TODAY
I'll escape into a book.

April 26

"Nothing makes one feel so strong
as a call for help."
George Macdonald

Don't be afraid to ask adults you know for help
or advice. Most will be honored and flattered
by your interest. You can even ask adults you
don't know personally but would like to learn
from. Want to find out what it's like to run a
newspaper? Write a letter to the publisher and
ask. Be sure to give your full name, your age,
and the school you go to. Or call the paper and
request an informational interview.

TODAY
I'll ask an adult for advice.

April 27

"Try breaking into your own home.
Most people find several ways
to get inside in just a few minutes."
Ray Johnson

Said by a security consultant (and former bur-
glar), these words might inspire you to check the
doors and windows at home. It's not a bad idea.
Neither is talking with your family (over dinner
tonight?) about ways to make your home safer.
Is everyone responsible about locking doors and
keeping track of their keys? Are emergency numbers posted near telephones? Are there enough
smoke detectors, with fresh batteries? Did you
know that you can ask local law enforcement for
a free home security survey?

TODAY
**I'll work with my family to make
our home more secure.**

EMPOWERMENT
ASSET #10: SAFETY

April 28

*"I think knowing what you can not do
is more important than knowing
what you can do."*
Lucille Ball

What are the laws in your community that
affect you? For example, how late can you stay
out before you're violating curfew? What if you
get into a fight? If you're caught tagging? If
you're at a loud party and the police are called
to break it up? If you cut class? Use a fake ID?
Make a crank call? Ignorance isn't bliss, it's just
ignorant. A lot of times, kids get into trouble
because they don't know they're breaking laws.
Being informed can help you make good decisions about what you should and shouldn't do.

TODAY
**I'll learn about the laws that affect
people my age.**

April 29

"We're witnessing a new revival
of religion."
Conrad Cherry

Teens are joining faith-based groups and prayer
circles, attending Christian rock festivals, doing
community service through faith-based organizations, hanging out in religious chat rooms,
even going to church and temple and mosque.
That may not surprise you (especially if you're
one of them), but it surprises a lot of baby-
boomer adults, maybe including your own parents. It's a good time to explore and express
your spirituality, because if that's what you
want to do, you've got a lot of company.

TODAY
**I'll get together with friends who share
my beliefs.**

April 30

"One great, strong, unselfish soul
in every community could actually
redeem the world."
Elbert Hubbard

Maybe you'll save the world. Maybe you
won't. But if you decide that at least part of the
reason you're here is to help other people, these
two quotes may inspire you in the years ahead:

- "Make one person happy each day and in
  forty years you will have made 14,600 human
  beings happy for a little time, at least."
  Charley Willey

- "If every American donated five hours a
  week, it would equal the labor of 20 million
  full-time volunteers." *Whoopi Goldberg*

TODAY
I'll help someone.

May 1

"Education is our passport to the future,
for tomorrow belongs to the people
who prepare for it today."
Malcolm X

A passport allows you to travel the world. An education allows you to travel through life with confidence. Sometimes it's hard to imagine how memorizing equations or reading Shakespeare or studying the skeleton of a frog or sitting through lectures about long-ago battles can possibly help you succeed in the future. It all seems so pointless. It's not. You're training your brain to understand and absorb new information. That's a skill you'll need no matter what you end up doing as an adult.

TODAY
I'll make good use of my time in school.

COMMITMENT TO LEARNING
ASSET #21: ACHIEVEMENT MOTIVATION

May 2

"Only your real friends will tell you
when your face is dirty."
Sicilian proverb

It's hard when a friend tells us something we
don't want to hear, especially when it's about
us. It's easy to get defensive and angry, to deny
or ignore what the person says, to pull away
and decide that maybe he or she isn't a friend
after all. To help ease the pain, we may turn to
people who don't know us as well or aren't as
honest. Try to see the other side: If it hurts for
you to hear something, it probably hurts for
your friend to say it. Honesty takes caring and
courage.

TODAY
I'll value friends who are honest with me.

May 3

"Bad conscience is a conscience
doing its duty."
Anonymous

There was something you were supposed to do,
but you didn't. Or something you weren't supposed to do, but you did. Either way, you don't
like the way you feel right now. You're uneasy,
maybe guilty, even ashamed. You wish you had
behaved more responsibly. The good news is,
it's not too late. If you can't do what you were
supposed to do, try something else—a positive
action that helps another person. Or apologize
for doing what you weren't supposed to do. See
if there's a way to make things right. Are you
troubled by something that happened far in the
past? Make amends if you can, then let it go.

TODAY
I'll listen to my conscience.

POSITIVE VALUES
ASSET #30: RESPONSIBILITY

May 4

"I don't feel like my money or my success defines me. I've always been very happy just bein' me."
Lauryn Hill

The Fugees singer and Grammy winner *(The Miseducation of Lauryn Hill)* knows what's important to her: family, integrity, giving back to the community, standing up for herself. In an industry dominated by men, she's writing songs, directing music videos, and producing albums. She's been called a "hip-hop groundbreaking genius." Yet she says, "I'm still trying to figure myself out, like most people…because I'm still living and learning." Check out the Refugee Project (www.refugeeproject.org), a nonprofit organization she founded that works to transform young people's lives.

TODAY
I'll be happy just being myself.

POSITIVE IDENTITY
ASSET #38: SELF-ESTEEM

May 5

"Trust is...very difficult to build
and very easy to destroy."
Thomas J. Watson Sr.

The older you get, the more freedom you want.
This makes your parents crazy because they
know how scary the world is, and what
they want is to keep you safe forever. You push;
they pull. You rebel; they get tough. You can
spend the next few years fighting with each
other, or you can make an effort to earn your
parents' trust. Be responsible, be honest, tell
them where you're going and who with, come
home by curfew, and keep your promises.

TODAY
I'll build my own trustworthiness.

BOUNDARIES AND EXPECTATIONS
ASSET #11: FAMILY BOUNDARIES

May 6

*"Inside you there's an artist
you don't know about."*
Jalal-Uddin Rumi

You may think you can't write, can't sing, can't act, can't paint, can't dance, can't draw, can't play music, and so on, but have you ever tried? There are only about a billion different ways to be creative, and unless you're the laziest, least imaginative person in the world, there's sure to be one that's right for you. If there's little or nothing available at your school, look around your community. Many towns and cities have arts organizations where you can get involved.

TODAY
**I'll give the artist inside me
a chance to come out.**

May 7

"Only I can change my life.
No one can do it for me."
Carol Burnett

If there's something you don't like about your life—your relationship with your family, your school performance, your group of friends, your job, the way you feel about yourself—what are you going to do about it? Whine, complain, blame other people, feel sorry for yourself, and hope that things will change? Or figure out how you can change them? What if you don't know where to start? Talk to an adult you respect—someone who seems like a good problem solver.

TODAY
I'll take the first step toward making a positive change in my life.

POSITIVE IDENTITY
ASSET #37: PERSONAL POWER

May 8

"The greatest oak was once a little nut
who held its ground."
Anonymous

When 1,000 students ages 13–17 were asked to name the worst influences facing today's youth, peer pressure was #2, right after drugs. Each day, you experience tremendous pressure to think, look, and act in ways that may or may not be right for you. Talk with your parents or other adults about your values and beliefs. What have you been taught? What decisions have you reached on your own? What are you still struggling with? Know what's important to you. This will give you strength to hold your ground against negative peer pressure.

TODAY
I'll sort out what's important to me.

SOCIAL COMPETENCIES
ASSET #35: RESISTANCE SKILLS

May 9

"Unless someone like you
cares a whole awful lot,
nothing is going to get better.
It's not."
Dr. Seuss

A family in New Canaan, Connecticut, decided
to show an elderly woman they cared about her
by cleaning up her yard and planting flowers.
The five children were so excited about the idea
that they told their friends. On the day of the
project, 15 kids showed up. That was the start
of Kids Care Clubs, now a national model for
other families, neighborhoods, communities,
congregations, and schools. You can start your
own Kids Care Club. To find out how, visit the
Web site (www.kidscare.org).

TODAY
**I'll learn about Kids Care Clubs
or another caring organization.**

POSITIVE VALUES
ASSET #26: CARING

May 10

"Development of one's mind is much more important than anything."
Bo Jackson

Until fairly recently, neuroscientists believed that your brain was fully developed by the time you reached puberty. Not true. Connections between your neurons are still being formed (zap! zing!) and your mind is still taking shape. Jay Giedd, a child psychiatrist at the National Institute of Mental Health (NIMH), believes that adolescence is the time when you "hard-wire" your brain to be better at certain things than others. What are you wiring your brain to be good at? Doing math...or watching TV? Music...or video games? Sports...or sitting around?

TODAY
I'll use my brain.

May 11

*"One has to grow up with good talk
in order to form the habit of it."*
Helen Hayes

Do you do your part to improve the communication in your family? Do you talk with your parents? If it's tough to start a conversation with them (maybe they didn't grow up with good talk?), try asking them about themselves. Nothing too personal—maybe a question about what things were like when they were your age, or how they feel about something on the news, or, if you're desperate, the weather. If you have brothers and sisters at home, talk with them. Help them form the good-talk habit.

TODAY
I'll talk with my family.

SUPPORT
ASSET #2: POSITIVE FAMILY COMMUNICATION

May 12

"If you have knowledge, let others
light their candles at it."
Margaret Fuller

If you have a skill, share it. You might tutor
younger kids in reading. Or help a neighbor
learn his way around the Web. Or show the kid
down the block how to fix her bike. Or teach
someone how to swim, take a good photo-
graph, bake an angel food cake, or raise tropi-
cal fish. By now, you probably have ideas of
your own. Anything you can do, you can pass
on to someone else. It's a win-win situation all
around.

TODAY
I'll be a teacher.

"'No' can be one of the most positive words
in the world. No, I will not be defeated.
No, I will not give up."
Martha Williamson

Are you having a hard time in school? Is there
a class that has you stumped? Do you wish you
hadn't signed up for Algebra II because it's just
too hard and you're spending hours every night
on homework and you don't have a life anymore? Try one more thing: Get help. Ask your
teacher if you can meet before or after school.
Find out if there's another student who can
tutor you. Explore all available alternatives. If
nothing works, see if you can transfer out of
that class and into another you'd rather take.
That's not giving up. That's choosing a different
way to succeed.

TODAY
I'll get help with a tough school subject.

May 14

"We must remember that one determined
person can make a significant difference,
and that a small group of determined people
can change the course of history."
Sonia Johnson

Want to make a difference in your school or
community? Maybe (who knows?) change the
course of history? Join a service club. Most
schools host clubs for students—like the Interact
Club (sponsored by Rotary International), Key
Club (Kiwanis), or Leo Club (Lions Clubs).
Some schools have their own clubs. If school
clubs aren't your thing, contact a national program that promotes youth service—like Youth
as Resources (www.yar.org) or Youth Service
America (www.ysa.org).

TODAY
**I'll join a service club or find another
way to serve.**

May 15

"It's only a piece of paper, but this little card
has kept millions of young people
off of drugs, out of gangs, and in school."
Denzel Washington

Oscar nominee Denzel Washington is talking
about the membership card to the Boys & Girls
Clubs of America. He believes that the Boys
Club of Mt. Vernon, New York, changed his
life and gave him a vision for achievement.
When a community values kids and teens, it
gives them safe places to go and positive things
to do. Is your community doing enough for
kids? Are there after-school programs, recreation programs, youth organizations? You
might volunteer to help at a program that
serves local kids.

TODAY
**I'll learn what my community is doing
for kids and teens.**

EMPOWERMENT
ASSET #7: COMMUNITY VALUES YOUTH

May 16

*"In every community, there is work to be done.
In every nation, there are wounds to heal.
In every heart, there is the power to do it."*
Marianne Williamson

No matter where you live, someone is hungry. Someone is poor, someone is lonely, someone is sick or neglected or abused. Every person, including you, can work for equality and social justice. Every effort, however small it may seem, has the potential to profoundly change someone's life for the better. Help support a relief organization or shelter. Write a check, join a local service organization, or find out how, when, and where you can volunteer in person.

TODAY
**I'll find a way to help others
in my community.**

May 17

> "No one is rich enough
> to do without a neighbor."
> *Danish proverb*

Some people live in the same houses or apartments for years and never get to know their neighbors. They don't have the time, or they have their own lives, or they're just not interested. If your neighborhood has a block or building party, why not go? You might find that the people across the street or down the hall are actually interesting. Take time to talk and you may discover shared interests, which can lead to friendship. At least you won't be strangers when you see each other again.

TODAY
I'll talk with a neighbor.

SUPPORT
ASSET #3: OTHER ADULT RELATIONSHIPS

May 18

"Many young Americans are making
a big difference in their communities."

Art Ryan

Art Ryan is chairman of the Prudential
Insurance Company of America. Each year,
Prudential joins with the National Association
of Secondary School Principals to sponsor the
Prudential Spirit of Community Awards, which
honor young people in grades 5–12 who have
helped make their communities better places to
live. If you need ideas or inspiration, you can
read about the latest honorees on the Prudential
Web site (www.prudential.com/community/
spirit/awards/).

TODAY

**I'll learn about kids and teens who are
serving their communities.**

May 19

"To know oneself is wisdom,
but to know one's neighbor is genius."
Norman Douglas

When people know each other, they're more likely to watch out for each other. That's not spying, that's caring, and it makes neighborhoods safer and more pleasant for everyone. If you don't know the people across the street or across the hall, make an effort the next time you see them. Say hi and introduce yourself. The time after that, spend a few minutes in conversation. Learn something about them and share something about yourself. You might even make new friends.

TODAY
**I'll introduce myself to a neighbor
I don't know.**

BOUNDARIES AND EXPECTATIONS
ASSET #13: NEIGHBORHOOD BOUNDARIES

May 20

"I'm a very spiritual person.
I have a strong belief in God,
who has completely led me to this point."
Christina Aguilera

According to a recent Gallup poll, 76 percent of teenagers believe that God plays an active role in their lives. Unless you attend a private religious school, your religious community may be separate from your school life. But that doesn't mean you can't live by your values and beliefs at school (or anywhere else). Let them guide you to do and be your best.

TODAY
I'll live according to my beliefs.

May 21

"If we don't change, we don't grow.
If we don't grow, we aren't really living."
Gail Sheehy

Part of your life's purpose is to change and grow. You won't stay the same forever—who would want to? You'll learn new things, meet new people, visit (and maybe live in) new places, have new experiences, and all of those things will change you and make you more than you are today. It's exciting to look ahead and imagine the kind of person you might become.

TODAY
I'll think of ways I've changed and grown over the past year.

POSITIVE IDENTITY
ASSET #39: SENSE OF PURPOSE

May 22

"One day, there will be no borders,
no boundaries, no flags and no countries,
and the only passport will be the heart."
Carlos Santana

If you know people of different cultural, racial, and/or ethnic backgrounds, you're lucky. If that's the way you like it, you're smart. You're not limited by ignorance or prejudice. You resist stereotyping people. You're more self-confident and comfortable in all kinds of situations. And your life is much more interesting than if you were surrounded by people just like you.

TODAY
**I'll enjoy the benefits of living
in a diverse world.**

SOCIAL COMPETENCIES
ASSET #34: CULTURAL COMPETENCE

May 23

"What lies behind us and what lies before us are tiny matters compared to what lies within us."
Ralph Waldo Emerson

Who are you really? What kind of person are you? What do you believe in? What's important to you? What would you stand up for, even if people you love disagreed with you, laughed at you, or gave you a hard time? Over the years, your opinions will change. Some of your beliefs may change. Things you care about now won't matter in the future, and things you haven't thought about yet will be incredibly important to you. But you'll always be guided by what's within you—your values, your beliefs, your self.

TODAY
I'll think about who I am.

POSITIVE VALUES
ASSET #28: INTEGRITY

May 24

"The brain is like a muscle. When it is in use
we feel very good. Understanding is joyous."
Carl Sagan

Think of homework as jogging for your brain.
Or skating, or skiing, or yoga, or weight training, or swimming, or aerobics, or whatever type
of exercise you most enjoy. Picture your brain
getting stronger and more flexible every day.
Imagine how good it will look in a bathing suit.
(A positive attitude makes homework easier,
and a sense of humor helps, too.)

TODAY
I'll exercise my brain.

May 25

> "Each human is a member of a community
> and should work within it."
>
> I Ching

If you want to live in a caring neighborhood, do your part to make it that way. Get to know your neighbors. Pick up trash on your street or in your building. Be polite and friendly to people of all ages, including slow old people and noisy little kids. If you can see that someone needs help—carrying groceries or crossing a street or getting a fully loaded stroller out the door or whatever—then offer to help. It only takes a few seconds to make someone's day.

TODAY
I'll be a caring neighbor.

SUPPORT
ASSET #4: CARING NEIGHBORHOOD

May 26

"The kids remember me and look up to me.
If you can let them know you care,
why wouldn't you want to?"

Al Leiter

New York Mets pitcher Al Leiter is talking about the kids in his hometown of Berkeley Township, New Jersey. So far, he's helped start a Big Brothers/Big Sisters chapter there. Plus he got behind a new ballpark for kids (complete with dugouts, landscaping, and an electronic scoreboard). He delivers meals to shut-ins and takes computers to schools in needy neighborhoods. After signing a 4-year contract in 1998, he pledged $1 million to charities. Look around at the kids in your community. How can you let them know you care? Teens can be role models, too.

TODAY
I'll be a role model to kids in my community.

May 27

"The race to grow up isn't worth running
if you're not alive at the finish line."
Maria Purdy

When you're 12 or 16 or 18, life stretches out
in front of you forever. You think you're invincible. You think you're immortal. You want to
try all kind of things—fun and daring and
dumb and wild. Eight percent of U.S. high
school seniors say they have tried Ecstasy, the
rave drug, at least once. Most have no problems. But Jason Austin in Florida and Kieran
Kelly in Ontario and Sam Buell in Wisconsin
took Ecstasy and died. Real names, real deaths.
Worth the risk?

TODAY
I'll stay alive.

Social Competencies
Asset #35: Resistance Skills

May 28

"When all else fails, read the instructions."
Anonymous

You're in trouble in school, and it's not the first time. Maybe you parked in the wrong spot or got caught surfing a certain Web site or said something that offended someone or handed out copies of an underground newspaper. But...but...you didn't know! If that's your excuse, give it up. Chances are your school publishes a student handbook. Read it. Pay special attention to the parts that cover school standards, student behavior, and sanctions (disciplinary actions). If your school doesn't have a handbook, this might be something you could help with. Ask a teacher for advice on getting started.

TODAY
I'll make sure I know the school rules.

May 29

"A strong, positive self-image is the best possible preparation for success in life."
Joyce Brothers

Sometimes we focus too much on the negative side of our personality traits, not enough on the positive side. Make a real effort to put a winning spin on who you are. Instead of thinking, "I'm too emotional," try thinking, "I'm in touch with my feelings." Instead of "I'm too shy," try "I'm reserved and thoughtful." Instead of "I'm too nosy," try "I'm curious and I love learning new things." Instead of "I'm too pushy," try "I'm assertive, and I get things done." And so on. It makes a difference.

TODAY
I'll see myself in the best possible light.

POSITIVE IDENTITY
ASSET #38: SELF-ESTEEM

May 30

"Loneliness and the feeling of being
unwanted is the most terrible poverty."
Mother Teresa

Think of a time in your life when you felt worse
than you ever thought possible. Really, really
down. Rock bottom. The pits. Why did you feel
that way? Because it seemed that you were
totally alone in the world? That no one cared
about you? That you might as well have never
been born? There are people everywhere who
feel that way right now. People in your state. In
your city or town or neighborhood. Maybe
someone next door or in the next room or the
chair right beside you.

TODAY
I'll reach out to someone who seems lonely.

May 31

"The most important single influence
in the life of a person is another person...
who is worthy of emulation."
Paul D. Shafer

In one national survey of kids ages 10–13,
43 percent said they had no role model. When
1,000 students ages 13–17 were asked to name
their biggest hero, 21 percent said "no one." If
you don't have at least one role model, do yourself a favor. Find one (or two, or three). Talk
with your parents about their role models. Who
did they look up to when they were your age?
Think about people you know—in your family,
school, community, youth group, religious
organization. There *are* people out there worth
admiring.

TODAY
**I'll try to find a role model among
the people I know.**

BOUNDARIES AND EXPECTATIONS
ASSET #14: ADULT ROLE MODELS

June 1

"People have discovered that they can fool the devil, but they can't fool the neighbors."
Edgar Watson Howe

If you think your neighborhood needs more boundaries—more standards for everyone to follow—then get together with your neighbors and make some. With your family and one or two others, host a block party, building party, or front-yard potluck. Go door-to-door and invite everyone. Then talk about neighborhood boundaries and identify three or more that everyone can agree on. For example: We agree to report suspicious activity. We agree to respect people and property. We agree to end parties by 11:00 P.M. Publish the boundaries in a one-page newsletter and distribute it around your neighborhood.

TODAY
I'll think about boundaries that would help our neighborhood.

June 2

"Every great mistake has a halfway moment, a split second when it can be recalled and perhaps remedied."
Pearl S. Buck

You're at a party having fun when someone hands you a beer, a pill, or a joint. Just like that. You take it almost without thinking. Now what? Is it too late to hand it back? Of course not. Will you feel kind of stupid? You might. Especially if the other person teases you or calls you a coward or a baby. Especially if other people notice and join in. Laugh it off and walk away. Or leave. Later, you won't feel stupid. You'll feel smart.

TODAY
I won't do anything that's not right for me.

POSITIVE VALUES
ASSET #31: RESTRAINT

June 3

"Youth are constantly told that they are
the hope of tomorrow.... We believe that
youth are the hope of today."
Steven A. Culbertson

Steven Culbertson is President and CEO of
Youth Service America, a resource center and
alliance of hundreds of organizations that give
teens opportunities to serve locally, nationally,
or globally. If you're looking for a way to serve,
go to YSA's Web site (www.ysa.org), type in
your Zip code, and you'll get a list of possibilities, complete with contact information. It's that
easy, it's that quick, and all you have to do is follow up with the organization that interests you.

TODAY
I'll find a way to serve.

EMPOWERMENT
ASSET #9: SERVICE TO OTHERS

155

June 4

"Read the best books first,
or you may not have a chance
to read them at all."
Henry David Thoreau

If you've got time on your hands this summer, think about reading a few great books. Serious books. Challenging books. Major works of fiction, nonfiction (history, biography, science, etc.), literature (novels, plays, poetry), spirituality, or whatever interests you. Ask a librarian or well-read friend or neighbor for recommendations. If it's noisy at home, do your reading at your local public library, where it's quiet and cool. Going back to school in the fall won't be such a shock, because you'll have kept your brain active and your thinking in gear.

TODAY
**I'll pick some great books to read
this summer.**

COMMITMENT TO LEARNING
ASSET #21: ACHIEVEMENT MOTIVATION

June 5

"Television has proved that people
will look at anything rather than each other."
Ann Landers

By the time you graduate from high school,
you'll have spent anywhere from 15,000 to
18,000 hours in front of the television. Why?
What's on? Try cutting down on the number of
hours you watch TV. Think about making one
day each week TV-free. Need an incentive?
When researchers studied 4,063 children and
youth ages 8–15, they found that those who
watched 4 or more hours of TV per day had
greater body fat and mass than those who
watched less than 2 hours per day.

TODAY
I'll keep the TV turned off.

CONSTRUCTIVE USE OF TIME
ASSET #20: TIME AT HOME

June 6

*"Doubt is part of all religion.
All religious thinkers were doubters."*
Isaac Bashevis Singer

Some young people drop out of their congregations during their teens. They start questioning organized religion and decide it's not for them. A religious community can be a strong, positive force in your life. Before you walk away (or even if you already have), talk with your youth leader, pastor, minister, rabbi, priest, or other spiritual leader. You're not the first teenager to have doubts. Chances are there's an adult who understands what you're going through and knows how to listen.

TODAY
**If I'm struggling with my spiritual beliefs,
I'll talk with an adult.**

June 7

*"Travel is more than the seeing of sights;
it is a change that goes on, deep and
permanent, in the ideas of living."*
Miriam Beard

Take every opportunity to travel that comes your way. Visit other neighborhoods, other cities, other states, other countries if you possibly can. Keep your eyes and ears and mind open. You'll discover that your ways aren't the only ways, your beliefs aren't the only beliefs, and the world isn't nearly as big as you think. If you can't go far, see what's available nearby. Are there celebrations of different cultures and religions? Festivals that honor ethnic holidays? Go and enjoy. You can also be an armchair traveler, thanks to books and videos.

TODAY
I'll travel or plan to travel.

June 8

"Winning has always meant much to me,
but winning friends has meant the most."
Babe Didrikson Zaharias

When we want to win—at sports, at school, a
contest or election, a prize or award—sometimes that's all we see. It's great to aim for a
goal and reach it, but try not to make that the
focus of your life. And try not to be the kind of
winner who treats other people like dirt on the
way to the top. Friends are important. Life is
lonely without them. Plus friends are the ones
who'll cheer the loudest when you win.

TODAY
I'll spend time with a friend.

SOCIAL COMPETENCIES
ASSET #33: INTERPERSONAL COMPETENCE

June 9

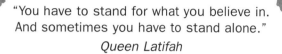

"You have to stand for what you believe in.
And sometimes you have to stand alone."
Queen Latifah

Wei Jingsheng spent nearly 18 years in Chinese prisons. He was tortured and forbidden to communicate with his family and friends. His crime? Anti-government writings calling for democracy. In 1997, he was expelled from China and sent into exile in the United States, where he continues to fight for human rights and democracy in his homeland. History is full of heroes like Wei who stood alone. Take time to learn more about them. Read their stories and their words. When you're called on to be courageous—when your beliefs are challenged—their examples may inspire you.

TODAY
I'll learn about a hero.

June 10

*"The best time to make friends
is before you need them."*
Ethel Barrymore

Is there someone you've noticed and would like
to know? Reach out. Don't wait for him or her
to make the first move. Say hi and smile. If the
time is right, try starting a conversation. Ask a
few general questions and really listen to the
answers. Be friendly and be yourself. See if you
have something in common. Maybe the interest
is mutual.

TODAY
**I'll take the first step toward
getting to know someone.**

SOCIAL COMPETENCIES
ASSET #33: INTERPERSONAL COMPETENCE

June 11

"Life's most persistent and urgent
question is, 'What are you doing for others?'"
Martin Luther King Jr.

Rephrase and personalize Dr. King's question as
"What am I doing for others?" or "What can I
do for others?" Then write it somewhere you'll
see it every day—in your planner, in a notebook
you're never without, on a Post-it stuck on your
computer. Each day, find a way to do something for another person. This can be a big deal
or a small, unexpected act of kindness. Make it
a habit and you'll change your life and maybe
someone else's, too.

TODAY
I'll do something for another person.

June 12

"If your friends jumped off a cliff,
would you?"
10,000,000 parents

That question belongs on any list of the Top 10
Stupid Things Parents Say (either right before
or right after "When I was your age…"). It
shows how little parents really know about
peer pressure. In fact, peer pressure isn't all
bad. In one study of 1,500 adolescents and
their families, researchers found that friends
were more likely to pressure each other to do
well than to do wrong. If your parents are in
the Peer-Pressure-Is-Evil camp, it's up to you to
set them straight.

TODAY
**I'll tell my parents about a time when
a friend helped me make a good decision.**

June 13

"The religious community is essential,
for alone our vision is too narrow to see
all that must be seen. Together, our vision
widens and strength is renewed."
Mark Morrison-Reed

Many young people today are spiritual seekers. They're exploring different belief systems and religious practices. They may attend one church for a while, then try another, sampling Buddhist meditation and Christian rituals and Kabbala (Jewish mysticism) along the way. Seeking is good, but it can get confusing. Sometimes it helps to be in a community of peers and adults who are sharing their beliefs, experiences, and questions. It's something to think about.

TODAY
**I'll consider joining a religious community
if I'm not already a member.**

June 14

"You can't have everything.
Where would you put it?"
Steven Wright

There's something you want, and you have the cash. Why not buy it? That $5 or $50 is burning a hole in your pocket. Here's a thought: Don't spend it. Use it to open a savings account if you don't already have one. That thing you want—will you still care about it next year or two years or five years from now? Saving isn't nearly as fun as going to the mall. But imagine your money growing into a nice little pile of cash—and future financial security for you.

TODAY
I'll save my money.

June 15

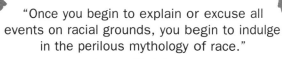

"Once you begin to explain or excuse all events on racial grounds, you begin to indulge in the perilous mythology of race."
James Earl Jones

Are you having issues with someone who happens to be of another race? You don't get along? You irritate each other? You sometimes face off and argue? Don't assume that your clashes are due to race. Some conflicts are labeled "racially motivated" or "race-based" when they're really just people problems—difficulties communicating or respecting each other that any two people might have, regardless of their race. The next time you and the other person tangle, try to see past skin color. What's really going on? Can you talk about it? Would it help to have a mediator?

TODAY
I'll look beyond race and focus on people.

June 16

"A small group of thoughtful people could change the world. Indeed, it's the only thing that ever has."
Margaret Mead

If there's a problem in your neighborhood or community that needs solving—not enough youth programs, too much crime and violence, pollution, graffiti, or anything else you notice—don't wait for someone else to solve it. Get together with other kids who feel the way you do. Brainstorm ideas. Find out who's good at what—doing research, making calls, writing letters to the editor. You'll make a bigger impact and get more done if you work as a team.

TODAY
I'll make a list of other kids who might want to help solve a problem.

EMPOWERMENT
ASSET #8: YOUTH AS RESOURCES

June 17

"Call it a clan, call it a network, call it
a tribe, call it a family. Whatever you call it,
whoever you are, you need one."
Jane Howard

Families can be challenging, inconvenient, and embarrassing. They can drive you crazy and make your life miserable. You may be eager to get away from your family—off to college or into your own apartment or just out of the house. These feelings are signs of your growing need for independence. They're perfectly normal. But whenever you think you can't take it anymore—whether it's Mom's complaining or Dad's bossiness or your sister's whining or your brother's rude table manners—take a deep breath, count to 10, and consider the alternative.

TODAY
I'll be thankful for my family.

June 18

"Opportunities pop up everywhere—
you just have to grab them."
Hannah Thomas

When kids and teens in Minneapolis, Minnesota, want to find something fun and positive to do, they call the What's Up? Youth Info Line. Created in 1996 by the Minneapolis Youth Coordinating Board (www.ycb.org), it connects young people ages 7–18 to youth programs in the area, from mentorships to sports and social activities. The staffers are teens from the Minneapolis Public Schools. If you live in Minneapolis, you can call (612) 399-9999. Or visit the Web site (www.whats up.org). What about starting a What's Up? line in your community?

TODAY
I'll find something fun and positive to do.

June 19

"I believe that we are solely responsible
for our choices, and we have to accept
the consequences of every deed, word,
and thought throughout our lifetime."

Elisabeth Kübler-Ross

Imagine that you could look into the future and
see the consequences of everything you do, say,
and think, starting today. This moment. Right
now. Would that make a difference? Would you
choose differently? Would you think before you
act or speak? Would you examine your
thoughts, values, and beliefs more closely?
Would you take more time to make decisions?
Try it and see how you feel by the end of the
day. Stronger? More secure? More mature?
More in control of your life?

TODAY
**I'll be responsible for what I do,
say, and think.**

June 20

"If Plan A isn't working, I have Plan B,
Plan C and even Plan D."
Serena Williams

No wonder Serena Williams is one of the top-ranked tennis players in the world. She's a super-planner. Most of us think we're doing pretty well if we have a detailed Plan A, maybe with a sketchy backup B for emergencies. But C and D? Maybe that's overkill...or maybe it's the way to success. If you have a goal that's very important to you—something you want to achieve more than anything else in the world—plan as much as you can.

TODAY
I'll plan to achieve a goal.

June 21

"A family is a place where minds come in contact with one another. If these minds love one another, the home will be as beautiful as a flower garden."

The Buddha

Maybe you've never pictured your home as a flower garden. Try it. Imagine a place that's peaceful and beautiful. Where you can relax and be yourself. Where you feel safe and secure. If your home is like that now, it's no accident. You've all worked hard to make it that way, and what you have is precious and rare. If the place where you live is totally not like that, can you think of ways to make it better? Spending time together is a start.

TODAY
I'll spend time with my family.

June 22

"Keep out of the suction caused
by those who drift backwards."
E.K. Piper

There's someone you've been friends with forever—maybe since you were little kids. Lately,
though, your friend has been making bad
choices. You want to be there for your friend,
and you still care, but you're worried that some
of those choices might affect you. Try talking
with your friend. See if he or she is willing to
listen and maybe get help. If not, it might be
time for you to back away. (If your friend is in
trouble, tell an adult.)

TODAY
I won't let anyone drag me down.

BOUNDARIES AND EXPECTATIONS
ASSET #15: POSITIVE PEER INFLUENCE

June 23

"I believe that each work of art, whether it is a work of great genius, or something very small, comes to the artist and says, 'Here I am.'"

Madeleine L'Engle

You're humming a tune and you don't know where it came from. There's music playing somewhere and your body wants to move. Or you notice that words are stringing themselves together in your mind. When art comes to you, pay attention. Hum your tune into a cassette recorder. Dance to the music. Write down the words. Do they want to turn into a poem, a rap, a story, or a play? If you don't have time right then to be creative, at least make notes so you don't lose your idea.

TODAY
If art comes to me, I'll welcome it.

June 24

"One man's ceiling
is another man's floor."
Paul Simon

The soda can you carelessly toss out a car window ends up in someone's yard. Or the music you blast from your stereo wakes up a neighbor's baby. It doesn't take that much effort to be thoughtful and considerate of others. Fight the stereotype of the rude, self-centered teen. Show by your actions that you're aware of and care about your neighborhood and the people around you.

TODAY
I'll be considerate.

June 25

"The only limits you really face are those you put on yourself."
Carmella House

You've heard of the power of positive thinking. Negative thinking is equally powerful. It can cripple your self-esteem, limit your choices, prevent you from taking the risks you need to grow and change, and keep you trapped in fear and uncertainty. If you're a negative thinker, make a deliberate, purposeful effort to change. Instead of "I can't," think "I'll find a way" or at least "I'll try." If you can't break out of your negative thinking, get help. Talk to an adult you trust.

TODAY
I'll think positively.

June 26

"Be like a postage stamp.
Stick to one thing until you get there."
Josh Billings

Persistence. Perseverance. Stick-to-it-iveness.
That's what will get you from point A to point
B, from wishful thinking to positive action,
from wanting to achieving. Can you think of
something you started, then dropped because
you got busy, distracted, or lazy? Is it something you care about enough to finish?
Something you'd better finish or else?
Something you may regret not finishing? Is this
a good day to wrap it up?

TODAY
I'll finish something I started.

SOCIAL COMPETENCIES
ASSET #32: PLANNING AND DECISION MAKING

June 27

"To maintain a joyful family requires much
from both the parents and the children.
Each member of the family has to become,
in a special way, the servant of the others."

Pope John Paul II

Are you doing your part to make your family supportive, even joyful? This isn't just about chores (although if you don't do your chores, who will?). It's about attitude, thoughtfulness, kindness, commitment—the emotional work of relationships. You're a servant when you choose to take your mom to a movie rather than go out with your friends. You're a servant when you stick up for your little sister. You're a servant when you ask your dad's opinion, then really listen to what he says.

TODAY
I'll be a servant to someone in my family.

June 28

"The greatest gift is the passion
for reading. It is cheap, it consoles, it distracts,
it excites, it gives you knowledge of the
world and experience of a wide kind."

Elizabeth Hardwick

Stuck at home with nothing to do? Read.
Worried or frustrated about events in your
life? Read. Need a lift or a pick-me-up?
Read. Feeling out-of-sorts, irritable, restless?
Read. Need something to take your mind off a
problem until you're ready to face it? Read.
These are all in addition to the usual reasons
for reading—to learn something, to flex your
brain, because you have to. Then again, you
don't really need a reason.

TODAY
I'll read for a reason or no reason.

COMMITMENT TO LEARNING
ASSET #25: READING FOR PLEASURE

June 29

"Be more concerned with your character
than with your reputation. Your character
is what you really are while your reputation
is merely what others think you are."
John Wooden

If you've ever been the victim of gossip, you
know how devastating it can be. One day
you're going along, living your life, and the
next you're the target of whispers and stares.
You may not believe it at the time, but the gossip will pass. Don't give in to it. Try not to let it
wear you down or put you on the defensive.
Your real friends will know the truth and stand
by you. Hold your head high and keep being
yourself.

TODAY
**I won't let gossip get to me—
and I won't gossip about other people.**

June 30

"Every family is a 'normal' family....
Wherever there is lasting love,
there is a family."
Shere Hite

If you've watched old TV shows on "Nick at Nite," you've seen plenty of so-called nuclear families: Dad, Mom, and their kids, living together in a house with a big yard. For many years, the nuclear family was held up as the ideal, and anything else was considered defective. Today, most people don't feel that way. Nuclear families, single-parent families, blended families, grandparent-run families, multigenerational families, foster families—whatever works is okay. Which means that families are free to be themselves.

TODAY
I'll enjoy my family.

SUPPORT
ASSET #1: FAMILY SUPPORT

 # July 1

"There is a close connection
between getting up in the world
and getting up in the morning."
Anonymous

It's summer. No school. Maybe no real reason
to get out of bed. So you sleep until 10 or 11 or
noon…. Hey bedhead! Find something to do. If
you can't get a job for whatever reason (you're
too young, all the jobs are taken), then volunteer. Help out at a local shelter. Read to people
in a nursing home. See if the Y could use a child
care assistant. Contact your local United Way
and ask what they need. Online, visit the Youth
Service America site (www.ysa.org) and enter
your Zip code to find opportunities in your
area.

TODAY
I'll get up.

July 2

"What wisdom can you find
that is greater than kindness?"
Jean-Jacques Rousseau

Kindness is really so simple. All it takes are two things: 1) being aware of other people, and 2) knowing they have feelings, wants, needs, sorrows, hopes, and dreams—just like you. It doesn't matter if they're older or younger than you, what gender or race they are, where they live, what they do, what school they go to, what political party they support, what football team they follow, how they look, what they wear, what they believe or don't believe. They deserve your kindness because they're human beings—just like you.

TODAY
I'll be kind.

POSITIVE VALUES
ASSET #26: CARING

July 3

*"A friend is one who walks in
when the rest of the world walks out."*
Walter Winchell

You've probably heard stories about successful people who took a fall and suddenly their friends disappeared. Or maybe you've seen it in real life—someone is popular one day, shunned the next. Many so-called friendships are based on things that don't really matter, like looks or status or money. If you want friends who will be there for you in good times and bad, choose them carefully. And be that kind of friend yourself.

TODAY
I'll be a loyal friend.

July 4

"Our kids earn what they get,
and that includes respect."
Woody Hayes

In one national telephone survey, more than 7 in 10 adults said that teens are "rude," "irresponsible," or "wild." If you want adults in your community to respect you, earn their respect. Be thoughtful, helpful, courteous, and kind whenever you get the chance. Be polite to adults you meet, even when they're less than polite to you. Be on your best behavior in public, and adults who usually stereotype teens might start thinking differently.

TODAY
I'll be polite to adults I meet.

EMPOWERMENT
ASSET #7: COMMUNITY VALUES YOUTH

July 5

*"Without a sense of caring,
there can be no sense of community."*
Anthony J. D'Angelo

It's hard to care about strangers. That's why it's important to know your neighbors. Bring some homemade cookies to the couple across the hall, spend a few moments talking, and you may learn that they like the same music you do. Say hi to the guy weeding his yard down the street and you may discover a shared interest in classic cars. Offer to walk a neighbor's dog and you could make two new friends—the neighbor and the dog. The more human contact you have, the more you care, the more connected you feel.

TODAY
I'll get to know a neighbor.

July 6

"A teenager who has spent a few hours
a week helping a younger child learn to read,
or spent a few hours at a hospice helping
an older person reach the end of their life
in dignity, is a changed person."
General Colin L. Powell

If you're not happy with yourself or your life, if you're frustrated or bored or blue and wondering why you're here and whether it even matters, here's a simple solution that works for almost everyone: Do something for another person. Volunteer. Lend a hand. Help. It's not that hard, anyone can do it, there are countless ways to do it, and the rewards are profound. Talk to teens who serve. Ask them why they do it. Don't be surprised if they tell you that their experiences have changed their lives.

TODAY
I'll start changing my life.

July 7

*"Thank goodness I had two parents
who loved me enough to stay on my case."*
Shaquille O'Neal

Right now, today, you might feel that your parents' rules are way too strict. If you want to get some perspective, try this: Think of two or three adults you know and respect—a neighbor, a coach, a youth leader, a grandparent, an uncle or aunt. Ask them what it was like when they were growing up. What were their parents' rules? Did those rules seem fair or unfair at the time? How do they seem now? Many successful adults credit their parents with putting them on the right path. Someday you may feel the same way about your parents.

TODAY
**I'll talk with adults about their
growing-up years.**

July 8

"I praise loudly. I blame softly."
Catherine II

You're with a group of friends, and one has just done something incredibly stupid. You know that real friends are honest with each other, so you don't want to just let it go. What's the best thing to do? If you have to say something right away, be as kind as you can. If it can wait until later, when you have the chance to talk privately, that's even better. When people feel attacked or cornered, they get defensive and don't listen.

TODAY
I'll be careful not to embarrass a friend.

SOCIAL COMPETENCIES
ASSET #33: INTERPERSONAL COMPETENCE

July 9

*"Creativity is inventing, experimenting,
growing, taking risks, breaking rules,
making mistakes, and having fun."*
Mary Lou Cook

Founder of the Santa Fe Living Treasures, a
program that honors elders in that New
Mexico city, Mary Lou Cook is a teacher, cal-
ligrapher, author, minister, craftsperson,
activist, tree planter, community leader, net-
worker, and volunteer who has made creativity
part of her everyday life. She once said,
"Anything that I do with my hands makes me
happy." Now in her 80s, she still teaches, cre-
ates, and officiates at weddings.

TODAY
I'll have fun being creative.

July 10

"Go get your crown, whatever that may be."
Debbye Turner

Debbye Turner is a veterinarian, a motivational speaker who has spoken to hundreds of thousands of students, and a cohost of *Show Me St. Louis,* a popular TV-magazine show. Before all that, she was the third black Miss America, crowned in 1990. It took seven and a half years and eleven tries in two states to get to the Miss America Pageant. Her goal: to win enough scholarship money to complete her education debt-free. Which she did. In May 1991, Debbye earned her Doctor of Veterinary Medicine degree from the University of Missouri.

TODAY
I'll think of ways to achieve something that's important to me.

POSITIVE IDENTITY
ASSET #39: SENSE OF PURPOSE

July 11

> "Do all the good you can
> By all the means you can
> In all the ways you can
> In all the places you can
> To all the people you can
> As long as ever you can."
>
> *John Wesley*

What if you took these words to heart? What if you read them, wrote them down, memorized them, and started and ended each day saying them to yourself? What if you actually lived these words? Imagine how your life would be transformed. Imagine the power you'd have to transform the lives of others. Maybe Wesley's words are too high to reach. Or maybe not.

TODAY
I'll do good.

POSITIVE VALUES
ASSET #26: CARING

July 12

> "Standing up for what you believe in
> is not always easy, but through perseverance
> you can accomplish your goal."
> *Andrew Leary*

Andrew Leary was 14 years old when he learned that hunger was a problem not only in other states, but in his own neighborhood. He led a two-and-a-half-year effort to establish the first permanent soup kitchen in his rural New Jersey community, and he helped raise $35,000 to run it. Called Harvest House, it was dedicated in October 1999. In February 2000, Andrew was named a Prudential Spirit of Community National Honoree. He learned that "even though I am a high school student, I have the vision and ability to change lives."

TODAY
I'll pursue a goal that will help others.

POSITIVE VALUES
ASSET #28: INTEGRITY

July 13

"When the newspapers have got nothing else
to talk about, they cut loose on the young.
The young are always news. If they are
up to something, that's news.
If they aren't, that's news too."

Kenneth Rexroth

When was the last time you saw a newspaper
article or TV news report that said something
good about kids and teens? Fight back against
teen bashing and trashing. If you're tired of
stories about kids in trouble, committing
crimes, acting out, or taking foolish risks, speak
up. Write a letter to the editor, or call TV or
radio stations. Ask them to feature more positive stories about teens.

TODAY
I'll speak out for kids and teens.

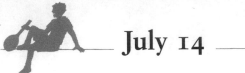

July 14

"Nobody ever died of laughter."
Max Beerbohm

Since laughter isn't fatal, it won't kill you to spend time with your family just having fun. What about watching comedies on video? (The older, the stupider, the sillier, the better.) Asking everyone to bring a joke to the dinner table? (Promise to laugh at your little sister's knock-knock jokes.) Sticking cartoons to the fridge with magnets? Setting aside a shelf or table as the place for joke books, cartoon books, and comic strips cut out of the newspaper? What about reading funny stories out loud? Or taking loony family Polaroids? What are other ways you can think of to loosen things up at home?

TODAY
I'll laugh with my family.

CONSTRUCTIVE USE OF TIME
ASSET #20: TIME AT HOME

July 15

"God enters by a private door
into every individual."
Ralph Waldo Emerson

What you believe is ultimately up to you.
Adults can teach you and guide you, but you're
the only one who knows what's in your heart
and mind. If that's true for you, it's also true
for other people, including those whose beliefs
may seem strange to you or wrong. Intolerance
leads to prejudice, discrimination, violence,
and hate crimes. Do your part to promote tolerance and acceptance in your community.
Show by example that you respect different
beliefs, even if you don't share them.

TODAY
**I'll be respectful of people whose beliefs
are different from mine.**

July 16

"Most people are willing to pay more
to be amused than to be educated."
Robert C. Savage

When was the last time you bought a movie
ticket, a bucket of popcorn, and a giant-sized
drink to wash it down? When was the last time
you bought a book? True, books cost money. A
hardcover bestseller might run you 30 bucks
(often less if you order online). Even paperbacks
are pricey. But buy a book (new or used) and it's
yours for as long as you want it. You can read it
again and again. You can underline your
favorite parts and write notes in the margins.

TODAY
I'll buy a book.

July 17

"Real glory springs from the silent
conquest of ourselves."
Joseph P. Thompson

You want to do it. You know you shouldn't.
And that makes you want it even more.
Everyone struggles with temptation; you're not
alone. A lot of people lose the struggle, but you
don't have to. Tell yourself that you're stronger
than whatever is tempting you. Promise yourself that you won't give in—at least not this
minute, this hour, this day. If a friend (or so-
called friend) is egging you on, avoid that person and hang out with someone else. Try to
surround yourself with people who will support
you in your decision.

TODAY
I'll be strong.

July 18

"Not all those who wander are lost."
J.R.R. Tolkien

No one is here by accident. Every life has a meaning. If you don't yet know the meaning of your life—if you're struggling to find purpose and direction—don't sweat it. Maybe what you're supposed to be doing right now is questioning, thinking, and exploring possibilities. You might ask yourself, "What matters to me? What gets me excited about each new day? What are my talents, interests, and skills? What do I want to learn? What dreams do I have for the future? If I could do only one thing with my life, what would it be?"

TODAY
I'll meditate on my purpose in life.

July 19

"Keep your promises to yourself."
David Harold Fink

What if your friends try talking you into something that's not right for you? Try this advice from author and educator Alex J. Packer: "Saying no is the ultimate act of personal control. When pressured to do something you don't want to do, simply respond with one of these phrases: 'No, thank you.' 'I'd prefer not to.' 'Count me out.' 'No can do.' Beyond that, you don't owe anyone an explanation.... You may discover that the minute one brave soul (namely you) says no, others will follow."

TODAY
I'll say no.

July 20

*"Optimism is something
you have to put effort into."*
Fran Shea

Some people are sunny by nature. The rest of us have to work at being optimistic—maybe a little, maybe a lot. Either way, it's worth it. Researchers have found that optimists have higher levels of natural killer-cell activity, which means that their bodies are better at fighting disease. They also have lower levels of cortisol, a stress hormone. Here's one way to become more optimistic: Whenever you catch yourself thinking negative, self-defeating thoughts, STOP. Force yourself to think positive thoughts instead. Retrain your brain to look on the bright side.

TODAY
I'll work on being more optimistic.

July 21

"To me old age is always fifteen years
older than I am."
Bernard Baruch

If most of your friends are the same age as you,
there's a simple reason for that. Starting in
kindergarten (or before), you've been lumped
together with your age group in school, sports,
and religious education. That will change
when you're an adult—but you don't have to
wait. You can form relationships now with
people of all ages. And your life will get a lot
more interesting.

TODAY
I'll expand my circle of friends.

July 22

"We gain the strength
of the temptation we resist."
Ralph Waldo Emerson

Every time you resist negative peer pressure,
every time you stand up for what you know is
right, every time you stay true to yourself and
your values, every time you don't give in or go
along makes you stronger. The first time you
say no is hard, especially if you're with people
you want to impress or a group you want to be
part of. The second time is easier. The third
time it's almost a habit. It's like weight training.
Each no is a rep that builds your resistance
muscles.

TODAY
I'll feel myself getting stronger.

July 23

"Music washes away from the soul
the dust of everyday life."
Berthold Auerbach

Music is a powerful mood-altering substance. It can make you happy when you're sad. It can help you relax when you're wired. It can sharpen your focus when you need to concentrate. It can fill you with delicious melancholy. It can take you to places you've never been. According to some studies, it can even make you smarter, or at least more receptive to learning. Music therapists use it for healing. Don't limit yourself to one kind of music. Listen to many kinds. If you can, make music of your own. Sing, play an instrument, compose, hum, or whistle.

TODAY
I'll make time for music.

CONSTRUCTIVE USE OF TIME
ASSET #17: CREATIVE ACTIVITIES

July 24

"The love of our neighbor in all its fullness
simply means being able to say,
'What are you going through?'"
Simone Weil

Floods, hurricanes, fires, and storms have a
way of bringing neighborhoods and communities
together. But it shouldn't take a tragedy for
people to ask "How are you?" and wait for an
answer. Take time to talk with a neighbor and
really listen. It might not be the most interesting
conversation you'll ever have, but it's guaranteed
to brighten his or her day. Take a little
extra time with those who have experienced a
recent illness or loss.

TODAY
I'll listen to a neighbor.

Support
Asset #4: Caring Neighborhood

July 25

"A lot of young girls have looked
to their career paths and have said
they'd like to be chief. There's been a change
in the limits people see."
Wilma Mankiller

From 1985–1995, Wilma Mankiller served as Principal Chief of the Cherokee Nation—the first woman in modern history to lead a major Native American tribe. (Her last name honors the high military rank achieved by a Cherokee ancestor.) Today she's a role model not just for young Native American women, but for anyone who has the good sense to study her example and learn from it. Your role model(s) don't have to be the same gender or race as you. A role model can be anyone you admire.

TODAY
I'll look for role models in new places.

July 26

"There's no place like home."
Dorothy in The Wizard of Oz

If you've seen the movie, you know that Dorothy clicked her heels three times and said those words to return home from Oz. Even a magical land full of witches and Munchkins was no substitute for her gray little Kansas farmhouse. Unless your home is very unhappy, you'll miss it when you're gone, which won't be that long from now. Make a special effort to notice things you like about your home. You may want to write down your thoughts and observations in a journal. Got a camera? Take some pictures.

TODAY
I'll appreciate where I live.

July 27

"I've always thought that you can think positive just as well as you can think negative."

Sugar Ray Robinson

You may have seen these glasses in a catalog or store: Halfway down (or up) each one is a line that circles the glass. Above the line is the word "Ottimista"—Italian for optimist. Below the line is the word "Pessimista." It's a literal translation of the question, "Is the glass half empty or half full?" You can choose how you want to see it. Which makes you feel sad, blue, gloomy? Which makes you feel happy, positive, hopeful?

TODAY
I'll choose to think positively.

July 28

"When I was growing up, our family was
so close it sometimes felt as if we were
one person with four parts."
Lee Iacocca

A study of 133 families found that youth who
have close relationships with their parents are
more likely to be emotionally healthy than
those who don't. The study also found that
being close to your family doesn't keep you
from becoming independent. Instead, it makes
you stronger and better able to be out on your
own. So don't feel that in order to grow up, you
have to distance yourself from your family.

TODAY
I'll bring my family closer.

Support
Asset #1: Family Support

July 29

"I firmly believe that none of us
in this world have made it until the least
among us have made it."

Oprah Winfrey

Maybe you define "making it" as earning a lot
of money, having a big house, driving an expensive car, and buying anything you want. To
someone else, "making it" means having
enough to eat. In the United States, more than
10 percent of all households were "food inse-
cure" in 1998, meaning they had to cut the size
of meals and skip meals. There's an organization somewhere in your town or city that works
to feed the hungry. Find it and help.

TODAY
I'll work to end hunger in my community.

July 30

"If each person sweeps in front of his or her own door, the whole street is clean."
Yiddish proverb

You're not responsible for anyone else's actions, words, thoughts, or feelings. You're only responsible for your own. Imagine what would happen if everyone knew that and lived accordingly. No more excuses. No more blaming or passing the buck. You can't make other people more responsible, but you can be a positive role model for your friends, brothers and sisters, neighbor kids, and other people who notice you and may follow your example.

TODAY
I'll model responsible behavior.

July 31

> "Some people give time, some money,
> some their skills and connections,
> some literally give their life's blood...
> but everyone has something to give."
>
> *Barbara Bush*

Former First Lady Barbara Bush has spent her life volunteering and supporting hundreds of charitable and humanitarian causes. In 1989, she founded the Barbara Bush Foundation for Family Literacy, which works to establish literacy as a value in every family in America. She's given her time, her money, her skills, and her connections to helping homeless people, people with AIDS, elderly people, and school volunteer programs. She calls herself "everybody's grandmother," but many people see her as an inspiration.

TODAY
I'll give something.

August 1

"If you tell the truth
you don't have to remember anything."
Mark Twain

Last week, you told your mom you were spending the night at a friend's house. You came home and talked about watching videos and staying up way too late. But you never really went to your friend's house. Instead, you went to a party. Now your mom wants to know more about one of the videos you mentioned. Without thinking, you reply, "Don't ask me. I've never seen it." Oops. You're busted.

TODAY
I'll be honest.

POSITIVE VALUES
ASSET #29: HONESTY

August 2

"No country that permits firearms
to be widely and randomly distributed
among the population...can expect
to escape violence."

Margaret Mead

No matter what side of the gun debate you're on, consider this: In one year, firearms killed no children in Japan, 19 in Great Britain, 57 in Germany, 109 in France, 153 in Canada, and 5,285 in the United States. And this: A gun kept in the home is 43 times more likely to kill a family member or friend than to stop a crime. The safest thing for your family is not to keep a gun in the home. If your family owns firearms, make sure they are safely stored.

TODAY
**I'll learn more about gun control
or gun safety.**

August 3

"The only thing that ever sat its way
to success was a hen."
Sarah Brown

Someone is encouraging you to learn, do, or try
something new. Don't just sit there. Get moving. Stretch yourself. Challenge yourself. Reach
out. Take a risk. If you don't, you'll never know
what you're really capable of. Maybe the other
person expects too much of you. Maybe you're
not in the mood to work hard at anything—it's
summer and school starts soon enough. Or
maybe this is just what you need to get out of
your summer laziness. Expectations can be a
burden or a boost. It's all a matter of attitude.

TODAY
I'll get moving.

BOUNDARIES AND EXPECTATIONS
ASSET #16: HIGH EXPECTATIONS

August 4

"Going to church doesn't make you
a Christian any more than going
to a garage makes you an automobile."

Billy Sunday

But going to church—or temple, or mosque, or any house of worship—makes you part of a religious community. And that's good for you, whether you're a believer or a struggler. Religious communities teach values that can help you through challenging times. Religious communities are caring and supportive. They have high expectations for young people that can bring out the best in you. Plus research has shown that teens who are involved in religious communities are less likely to get in trouble with alcohol, drugs, or other risky behaviors.

> # TODAY
> **I'll appreciate the good things
> religious communities do.**

CONSTRUCTIVE USE OF TIME
ASSET #19: RELIGIOUS COMMUNITY

August 5

"I've never felt celebrity status
automatically makes you a role model.
It's personal values, morals, and ethics—
not money and status."

Joe Dumars

It's easy to choose celebrities as role models.
They're everywhere (in movies, on TV, in
advertisements), plus they're glamorous, successful, rich, attractive, and seem to have it all.
Before you start looking up to famous people—
athletes, movie stars, rock stars, models—learn
more about them. How do they live their lives?
What do they do for others? Do they set a good
example? Are they worth looking up to?

TODAY
I'll learn more about a celebrity I admire.

BOUNDARIES AND EXPECTATIONS
ASSET #14: ADULT ROLE MODELS

August 6

"There are homes you run from,
and homes you run to."
Laura Cunningham

Ask your parents if they'd be willing to participate in the McGruff House Safety Program.
This national program establishes neighborhood homes as places where children who are
threatened, hurt, or lost can go for help. To find
out more, contact the National Crime Prevention Council, (202) 466-6272 (www.ncpc.org).
Even if your home isn't an official McGruff
House, it can still be a safe house, known as a
place that helps and welcomes kids.

TODAY
**I'll talk with my parents about
making our home a safe place for kids.**

August 7

> "Girlfriends are the best thing
> that ever happened to this planet."
> *Natalie Cole*

Okay, guy friends too. But whether you're a girl or a boy, it's good to have close friends of the same gender. Friends you can hang out with, be yourself with, talk to, and get advice from. Friends you can call to go to the mall or watch the game. Especially if you spend a lot of time together, make sure that your friends are good for you—and you're good for them. Pressure each other to stay on track and out of trouble.

TODAY
I'll be a good influence on my friends.

BOUNDARIES AND EXPECTATIONS
ASSET #15: POSITIVE PEER INFLUENCE

August 8

"The true measure of an individual is
how he treats a person who can do him
absolutely no good."
Ann Landers

Visit Amnesty International's Web site
(www.amnesty-usa.org), click on "Act Now!"
and you'll learn about several letter-writing
campaigns you can join. A few recent issues:
alleged abuses in U.S. jails, a humanitarian cri-
sis in a Middle Eastern country, children forced
to become soldiers in an African war. If you
write a letter (or more than one), will you ever
hear back from the person or persons you may
have helped? Doubtful. Will anyone come to
your door and say thank you? No. Is it worth
doing anyway? You decide.

TODAY
**I'll help another person without expecting
anything in return.**

August 9

"There is much pleasure to be gained from useless knowledge."
Bertrand Russell

So maybe you don't need to know the history of comic books. Or what happened 250 million years ago that caused 85 percent of the species in the sea to vanish. Or when the tug-of-war was dropped from the Olympic games (did you even know it had been part of the Olympic games?). Or how the lead gets into a pencil. But wouldn't it be fun to know? Follow your curious nose to the nearest library or bookstore. Tip: Look for books by Charles Panati *(Panati's Extraordinary Origins of Everyday Things)* and Caroline Sutton *(How Do They Do That? Wonders of the Modern World Explained)*.

TODAY
I'll learn something useless.

COMMITMENT TO LEARNING
ASSET #25: READING FOR PLEASURE

August 10

"It isn't walls and furniture that make
a home. It's the family."
Natalie Savage Carlson

Maybe you live in a big, fancy house with a
room full of expensive toys. Maybe you live in
a cramped apartment, share a room with other
family members, and don't have much to call
your own. There's a lot of pressure these days
to have the latest, greatest things and the status
that goes along with them. Do you feel loved
and supported at home? Are there people you
can talk to? People who will listen? Someone
who will sit with you when you're feeling
blue—someone who can always make you
laugh? If you do, you have a lot.

TODAY
I'll focus on what really matters.

*"My mother outlined a code of conduct
and strictly enforced it, to try to protect us."*
Jackie Joyner-Kersee

Winner of six medals in four Olympic games,
voted the greatest female athlete of the 20th
century, Jackie Joyner-Kersee realizes that her
mother wasn't only trying to keep her children
safe. "Her rules served an additional purpose,"
she says. "She was determined to put us on the
path to a better life by teaching us to be disci-
plined, hardworking, and responsible." What
do you think your parents want for you?

TODAY
**I'll ask my parents about their hopes
for my future.**

"Sex is a part of yourself that you
should never give away on a whim."
Sheneska Jackson

Teens are having sex earlier. National surveys
report that sexual activity is declining among
all teens—except those under age 15.
According to the 1999 Youth Risk Behavior
Survey (developed by the Centers for Disease
Control and Prevention and made available to
all school districts), 8.3 percent of students
report having had sex before age 13. On the
other hand: A majority of both girls and boys
who are sexually active (8 in 10 girls, 6 in 10
boys) say they wish they had waited until they
were older to have sex.

TODAY
I won't give myself away.

August 13

"People who cannot find time
for recreation are obliged sooner or later
to find time for illness."
John Wanamaker

You are responsible for your own health. For now, your parents can make sure you get your shots and see the dentist. But that's just maintenance. You're the one who needs to put down the remote or game controller and move those bones of yours. Are you on a team or two? Do you visit the gym? Do you walk or run or bike or blade or ski or swim or play tennis or shoot hoops? Look around at the out-of-shape adults you know. Let them inspire you to get fit and stay fit.

TODAY
I'll make time for exercise.

POSITIVE VALUES
ASSET #30: RESPONSIBILITY

August 14

"My grandmother taught me to count
my blessings. There's always an upside
to whatever bad happens."
Chamique Holdsclaw

What have your grandparents taught you?
(Besides funny stories about what your parents
were like when they were kids.) If you're lucky,
your grandparents are part of your life and you
get to see them often. Even if you live too far
apart to visit more than once a year or so, stay
in touch by phone, snail mail, or email.
Relationships with grandparents are special.

TODAY
**I'll talk to my grandparent(s) or remember
them if they aren't alive anymore.**

> "Parents who are afraid to put their
> foot down usually have children
> who step on their toes."
> *Chinese proverb*

Even famous teens have rules to follow and parents who mean business. When actor Zachery Ty Bryan was 15, he had a weekend curfew. On weekends and weeknights, he had to call his parents and tell them where he was. When Michelle Kwan was 16, she wasn't allowed to drive her new Jeep without one of her parents in the car. Kellie Martin remembers that when she was starring in the TV series *Life Goes On,* her parents and publicist "watched her like a hawk."

TODAY

**I'll know I'm not the only one
who has to follow rules.**

BOUNDARIES AND EXPECTATIONS
ASSET #11: FAMILY BOUNDARIES

August 16

"I haven't a clue as to how my story
will end. But that's all right. When you set out
on a journey and night covers the road, you
don't conclude that the road has vanished....
And how else could we discover the stars?"

Anonymous

You can't predict everything that will happen in
your life. Even the most detailed plans can fall
apart. Maybe you won't get into the college
you're determined to go to. Or once you get
there, you'll wish you were somewhere else.
Maybe you won't end up in the career you're
dreaming of today. Or you will, but you won't
like it. It's possible, even likely, that your life
will turn out completely different from what
you imagine. Keep an open mind, keep moving,
and trust that things will turn out okay.

TODAY
I'll be open to surprises.

"I wasn't as nice a guy as I should have been all the time…. And I don't have any excuses for that. I do have an explanation, though—fear and ignorance."

LL Cool J

Are you afraid of being too nice? Too caring? Do you think your friends will see you as a softy, a sucker, a chump? Or maybe they'll think you're trying to show them up by acting superior. Either way, it could be hard for you, especially if your friends think it's cool to be cold. You'll have to decide what's important to you and what kind of person you are.

TODAY
I'll look at my own behavior. Am I nice or not?

POSITIVE VALUES
ASSET #26: CARING

August 18

"The best inheritance a parent can give
to his children is a few minutes
of their time each day."
M. Grundler

If your parents are willing to give you their time, take as much as you can. Even if you'd rather watch TV or talk on the phone or surf the Web or go out with your friends. In a national study, almost 20 percent of 6th–12th graders said they hadn't had a good conversation with either of their parents in more than a month. Ideas for times and places to talk: In the car on the way to the mall. At the dinner table. While walking the dog. During commercials. Before bed, even if you're just stalling.

TODAY
I'll spend time with my parents.

CONSTRUCTIVE USE OF TIME
ASSET #20: TIME AT HOME

August 19

"What its children become,
that will the community become."
Suzanne La Follette

Talk to almost any adults about teens today, and they'll probably say that kids used to be more respectful, more responsible, and more polite. Maybe it's true. You can't change other people's behavior, but you can check your own and see how it rates. You can be the teen in your neighborhood who doesn't litter, doesn't swear, helps out, and has good manners. Adults will appreciate it, and other kids may notice and decide to try it themselves.

TODAY
I'll set a good example in my neighborhood.

August 20

"Life is about not knowing, having
to change, taking the moment and
making the best of it, without knowing
what's going to happen next.
Delicious ambiguity."

Gilda Radner

You have so much to look forward to in the
coming months and years and decades—including things you can't possibly predict or imagine
today. It's normal and natural to worry about
your future, to wonder what you'll be doing
after you finish school and what your life will
be like (where will you live? where will you
work? will you be alone or with someone? and
on and on). But the truth is, almost anything
can happen. Life is full of surprises.

TODAY
I'll be excited about my future.

August 21

"Mitakuye Oyasin."
Lakota saying

Say *Mee-tah-koo-yay O-yah-seen*. Translated, the phrase means "All my relations." Among the Lakota Sioux people, it's a greeting, a blessing, a belief, and a prayer of oneness and harmony. It's also a reminder that we are all related—to each other and to all forms of life on Earth. We're not limited to our immediate or extended families. We're part of the human family, and beyond that, the family that includes and embraces every living thing. We're all brothers and sisters.

TODAY
**I'll meditate on what it means
to be related to every living thing.**

POSITIVE VALUES
ASSET #27: EQUALITY AND SOCIAL JUSTICE

August 22

*"Freedom's just another word
for nothin' left to lose."*
Kris Kristofferson

What would your life be like with no rules, no restrictions, no one to watch over you? Maybe you're feeling trapped by the limits and boundaries your parents have set. Try to look on the bright side. Life without limits is chaos. Rules guide us in making good decisions and provide a structure for our lives. In a national survey of more than 218,000 students in grades 6–12, some said they had too much freedom.

TODAY
**I'll try thinking of limits as positives
rather than negatives.**

August 23

"What sane person could live in this world
and not be crazy?"
Ursula K. LeGuin

Hunger, poverty, crime, violence, wars, torture, abuses, cruelty, greed, indifference, disasters, diseases, death—it's too much. Too depressing. Think about it all the time and you'll go crazy. Think about it for part of the time, talk about it with other caring, compassionate people, and you may decide to do something about one small part of the world's big problems. Every positive action, every major change begins with one person who has an idea and acts on it. You might have your own idea, or you might join an organization or cause that's already up and running.

TODAY
**I'll do something to make the world
a better place.**

POSITIVE VALUES
ASSET #27: EQUALITY AND SOCIAL JUSTICE

August 24

"You create your opportunities
by asking for them."
Patty Hansen

If you want to play a useful role in your community, don't wait to be invited. Volunteer your time, talents, and abilities. Identify something you think needs changing, then work to change it. Lobby for (or against) ordinances or laws. Help create or update a community or neighborhood Web page. Campaign for a candidate whose ideas you believe in. Side benefit: Life becomes more interesting when you're out in the world.

TODAY
I'll make myself useful.

August 25

*"Our identity is continuously reformed
and redirected as we move
through a sea of changing relationships."*
Kenneth J. Gergen

From daycare providers to teachers, coaches, counselors, and youth leaders, other adults besides your parents have a powerful influence on your life. Is there anyone you'd like to thank for being especially kind or helpful? Anyone from your past you'd like to get back in touch with? That person might love to hear from you. Even if you haven't communicated in years—even if one of you has moved—you might be able to find him or her by doing an Internet search.

TODAY
**I'll contact an adult I used to know
who was important to me.**

SUPPORT
ASSET #3: OTHER ADULT RELATIONSHIPS

August 26

*"The world's children deserve
to walk the earth in safety."*
President Bill Clinton

Caring neighborhoods are safer neighborhoods. A study of 343 neighborhoods in Chicago found lower rates of violence in urban neighborhoods where there's a strong sense of community and values. Work with your parents, other adults, and your friends in the neighborhood to plan a block party or building party, potluck dinner, or neighborhood cleanup. If your neighborhood doesn't have a watch program, offer to help start one. Learn how from the National Crime Prevention Council (www.ncpc.org).

TODAY
I'll make my neighborhood a safer place.

SUPPORT
ASSET #4: CARING NEIGHBORHOOD

August 27

"Other people may not have had high
expectations for me…but I had high
expectations for myself."
Shannon Miller

Winner of seven Olympic medals and nine
World Championships medals, Shannon Miller
is America's most decorated gymnast. It hasn't
been easy. As a baby, she wore braces because
her legs weren't growing properly. She fell off
the balance beam during a major competition in
1987. A knee injury kept her out of the 2000
Sydney Olympics. Her Oklahoma hometown
newspaper, the *Edmond Sun,* called her "a wonderful example of attributes all of us should
model: discernment, wisdom…enthusiasm, self-
control, diligence, patience…determination,
boldness, resourcefulness, and decisiveness."

TODAY
I'll have high expectations for myself.

BOUNDARIES AND EXPECTATIONS
ASSET #16: HIGH EXPECTATIONS

"Stand up for the things that are right.
Try to talk things out instead of fight."
Robert Alan

Being peaceful doesn't mean never having conflicts. It means knowing how to resolve conflicts without using hurtful words and physical force. The next time you tangle with someone, give yourself a day to cool down, if you can. Then talk about what happened. Talk about the events that led up to the conflict. Talk about how you feel. Ask the other person to talk about how he or she feels. Really listen. Try to understand the other person's point of view. Come up with solutions together. Agree on one to try. Then try it. If that solution doesn't work, choose another.

TODAY
I'll talk through a problem I'm having with another person.

August 29

"Over the long run, superior performance depends on superior learning."
Peter Senge

The more you learn, the more you know, the more you can do, and the more choices you have in life. It's a simple equation and it's not even math. When someone offers to teach you a skill you don't have, say yes. If your parents want to take you to a concert, a play, or an art exhibit, go. If a class sparks your interest, sign up. If a book looks interesting, read it. If you're curious about something, pursue it. Never turn down a chance to learn, even if you're not sure what good it will do you.

TODAY
I'll learn something.

COMMITMENT TO LEARNING
ASSET #21: ACHIEVEMENT MOTIVATION

"Do not look where you fell,
but where you slipped."
African proverb

Maybe you've done something you're not proud of. Something that goes against your values. Something you wish you hadn't done. You can beat yourself up and decide you're a loser, which will only make you feel worse. Or you can figure out why you did it and how to avoid a repeat performance. Regret makes you weak and traps you in the past. Planning makes you strong and prepares you for the future.

TODAY
**I'll look at where I slipped—and plan
not to slip again.**

August 31

"Honesty is something
that never wears out."
Waylon Jennings

Think about your friends. They probably fall into categories—people you like to hang out with, people you have things in common with, people you like to talk to. Is there someone you can count on to be honest with you no matter what? Not someone who constantly criticizes you and brings you down. That's not a friend. You need at least one person in your life who will let you know when you've made a bad choice, hurt someone else, gone too far, or seem headed in the wrong direction.

TODAY
I'll thank a friend for being honest with me.

SOCIAL COMPETENCIES
ASSET #33: INTERPERSONAL COMPETENCE

September 1

"Service to others is the rent you pay
for your room here on earth."
Muhammad Ali

Make A Difference Day, sponsored by *USA
Weekend* magazine and the Points of Light
Foundation, is a great way to find out how it
feels to volunteer. In 1999, 2 million people in
hundreds of towns accomplished thousands of
projects and helped an estimated 22 million
people. This special day happens on the fourth
Saturday of every October. To find out how you
can get involved, call the Make A Difference
Day Hotline, (800) 416-3824. Or visit the Web
site (www.makeadifferenceday.com).

TODAY
I'll plan to serve.

September 2

"We are a community…a family."
High school vision statement

A community with locked doors, security guards, and metal detectors. A family that greets guests with signs saying "All Visitors Must Check In At The Office. Trespassers Will Be Prosecuted." Some schools are among the least welcoming, most unfriendly places on earth. No wonder parents stay away. To get parents more involved, you may need to make your school more family-friendly. Got any ideas? Share them with teachers; share them with your principal.

TODAY
I'll work to make my school more family-friendly.

SUPPORT
ASSET #6: PARENT INVOLVEMENT IN SCHOOLING

September 3

> "Motivation is a fire from within. If someone
> else tries to light that fire under you,
> chances are it will burn very briefly."
>
> *Stephen R. Covey*

To succeed in school (and in life), you need to be motivated from the inside, not the outside. Rewards (like parents who pay you for A's) and punishments (or ground you for D's) are external motivations. For each class you're taking, try to find a reason inside yourself for showing up and doing the work. Maybe what you're learning will be useful in the future. Maybe you like learning new things. Maybe that class is the only one you have with someone you're crazy about.

TODAY
I'll be motivated from the inside.

September 4

"Too often we underestimate the power of a touch, a smile, a kind word, a listening ear, an honest compliment, or the smallest act of caring, all of which have the potential to turn a life around."
Leo Buscaglia

Be a caring person today. Wherever you go, whatever you do. At home, be more pleasant and helpful. Do small acts of kindness at school. Smile at people you see in your neighborhood and community. Hold a door or help carry a bag of groceries. Make a phone call, write a letter, or send an email to someone who'd love to hear from you. Offer to babysit a neighbor's kids for an hour. Serve at a soup kitchen. Come up with your own idea, then just do it.

TODAY
I'll make a difference in someone else's life.

POSITIVE VALUES
ASSET #26: CARING

September 5

"I believe in rules. Sure I do. If there
weren't any rules, how could you break them?"
Leo Durocher

Do some of your school's rules seem lame and
outdated? Don't just decide to break them. (If
the rules are still in force, so are the consequences.) Instead, you might try to improve
them. Get together with other students who feel
the same way you do. Arrange to meet with a
teacher who's known for having an open mind.
Find out what other schools in your community or state are doing. Make a plan and talk to
your principal.

TODAY
**If I think a school rule needs improving,
I'll work to make it better.**

September 6

"If you are planning for one year, grow rice.
If you are planning for 20 years, grow trees."
Chinese proverb

Taking easy classes because you need credits to
graduate is growing rice. Taking more challenging classes because you want to learn how to
learn is growing trees. It's hard to look ahead
when your life is full of school and friends and
family and responsibilities. If you can, take a
few minutes each day (or week) to get very quiet
and think a year ahead, or five years, or even
farther. How many of the decisions you're making now have the power to shape your future?
Are you growing rice or trees?

TODAY
**I'll spend a few minutes of quiet time
thinking about my future.**

SOCIAL COMPETENCIES
ASSET #32: PLANNING AND DECISION MAKING

September 7

"Life is like a dog sled team. If you ain't
the lead dog, the scenery never changes."
Lewis Grizzard

If you think school is boring, maybe you need a
change of scenery. Instead of being a follower,
be a leader. You might run for student council,
join a committee, direct a play, or start a new
club. Some students serve on parent-teacher
association (PTA) or organization (PTO) boards.
Some schools have formed PTSAs (parent-
teacher-student associations). Get involved, get
active, and school will get more interesting.

TODAY
I'll explore ways to be a leader at school.

September 8

"The wisest mind has something
yet to learn."
George Santayana

Maybe you've got your future all planned out.
You want to work with computers, or fly jets, or
play pro basketball, or be a pediatrician, or...?
Anyway there you are, stuck in English class
and forced to read an old novel by a dead writer
that has no connection whatsoever with your
goals. Try not to hate it too much. It may be
hard to see right now, but nothing you learn is
ever wasted. Just the process of learning something new is good for your brain.

TODAY
I'll keep my mind open to learning.

September 9

"Where the school shows that it cares,
the students care."
Jerome Bruner

Does your school care? Do you think it cares? What do other people think? It's not hard to find out. Survey the students in your school. Survey the teachers, too. Ask, "Do you think our school is a caring, encouraging place to be? Why or why not?" Ask people to give examples of ways your school is and isn't caring. Invite suggestions on ways to make it better. Then form a committee of students, teachers, and administrators to act on some of the suggestions.

TODAY
I'll help to make my school more caring.

September 10

"Tell everyone what you want to do
and someone will want to help you do it."
W. Clement Stone

Talk about your life goals, hopes, priorities, and dreams. Talk with your parents. Talk with your friends. Talk with other adults you trust and respect. Ask for their advice and insights. Ask if they know ways you might reach your goals, or people who might help you. Identify adults in your community who are doing what you'd like to do someday. See if they'll agree to meet and talk with you. Learn how they got where they are and ask for pointers. No one is successful in a vacuum. Everyone needs guidance—and good connections.

TODAY
**I'll talk with other people
about what I want to do with my life.**

POSITIVE IDENTITY
ASSET #39: SENSE OF PURPOSE

September 11

"It wasn't raining when Noah built the ark."
Howard Ruff

You plan to get together with friends. You plan a party. Maybe you plan to graduate from high school and go to college. Most of the plans we make are things we look forward to. What we don't plan for are the sudden, surprising, not-so-pleasant turns that life can take. What if you don't get into a class you want? What if you don't get asked to the dance, or the person you ask says no? What if you don't get the part-time job you need to earn money for a car or college? All kind of plans are powerful, even the ones that aren't much fun.

TODAY
I'll plan for a rainy day.

September 12

"Life is like a ten-speed bike.
Most of us have gears we never use."
Charles Schulz

Are you happy with how you spend your time outside of school? Are you involved in activities you find stimulating, challenging, meaningful, fun? Are you learning new things, discovering new talents? Do you have close, caring relationships with adults besides your parents and maybe your teachers? Are you connected with other kids who share your interests? If you can't answer yes to all or most of these questions, consider joining a youth program, team, club, or organization. More than 17,000 national and local youth organizations operate in the United States today. There's bound to be one that's right for you.

TODAY
I'll get in gear.

CONSTRUCTIVE USE OF TIME
ASSET #18: YOUTH PROGRAMS

September 13

"Once you get people laughing,
they're listening and you can
tell them almost anything."
Herbert Gardner

Want to make and keep friends? Cultivate a sense of humor. You don't have to wear a clown nose or tell jokes on the school bus every day. But especially if you're on the serious side, try lightening up a little. Go to funny movies. Watch funny videos. Share funny stories. Laugh when your friends say funny things. Laughter is good for you, too. It makes you feel better and might even make you healthier. Studies suggest that laughter decreases the level of stress hormones in your body and increases production of disease-fighting chemicals.

TODAY
I'll work on my sense of humor.

September 14

"Integrity is not a conditional word.
It doesn't blow in the wind or change
with the weather. It is your inner image
of yourself, and if you look in there
and see a man who won't cheat,
then you know he never will."

John D. MacDonald

Sometime today, take a few minutes for yourself. Go somewhere you won't be interrupted or distracted. Then think—really think—about yourself. Do you know what you believe in? What you stand for? What you won't stand for? What your personal values are? You're still growing and changing. You're not supposed to be finished or perfect. But you should have a good idea of who you are. What if you don't? Talk with an adult you trust.

TODAY
I'll look inside myself.

POSITIVE VALUES
ASSET #28: INTEGRITY

September 15

"Free speech carries with it some freedom to listen."
Warren E. Burger

Schools are considering all kinds of new rules. In some schools, these rules are already in place. Like no backpacks, or clear backpacks only. School uniforms. Random drug testing. Random locker searches. Closed campuses (students must stay on campus during the whole school day). No tank tops. And so on. If there's a rule you don't agree with, you can try to change it. Talk with your teachers, your principal, or the student council. But don't just talk. Listen. Maybe there's a good reason for the rule.

TODAY
I'll get the facts about school rules.

September 16

"I know I could fight and really hurt someone, but I know now that I don't need to."
Chanel Barboza-Owens

When Chanel was growing up, she heard two views of dealing with violence. Some of her family members pushed her to be a fighter. "You're big; use your size. If anybody gets in your way, just hit 'em." Others told her, "Violence is inappropriate. You have to do it another way." A teacher encouraged her to get the right perspective and help other people in her community. Chanel was 17 when she told her story to the *Christian Science Monitor*, hoping to inspire other teens to choose a better way.

TODAY
I'll surround myself with people who resolve conflicts peacefully.

SOCIAL COMPETENCIES
ASSET #36: PEACEFUL CONFLICT RESOLUTION

September 17

"It's easy to hate a stereotype,
hard to hate someone you know."
Lynn Duvall

Maybe you think all Mexicans are illegals. Or all Arabs are terrorists. Or all African-Americans are lazy. Or all whites are racist. Or all Asians are—what? Shifty? Secretive? Good at math? Do you actually know a Mexican or an Arab or an African-American or a white or an Asian as a friend? If your answer is no, then you don't know anything about the people you're stereotyping. And in a world that's growing more diverse by the minute, ignorance is a barrier to success.

TODAY
I'll take the first step toward getting to know someone of a different cultural, racial, and/or ethnic background.

September 18

"A school without football is in danger
of deteriorating into a medieval study hall."
Frank Leahy

Schools need football (and other athletics). They
need music, art, physical education, gifted education, and other so-called "special" programs
that are often the first to go when budgets get
tight. If your school is cutting back, speak up.
Circulate a petition and get signatures from
other students, teachers, and parents who feel
the way you do. Brainstorm ways to fundraise
to keep programs alive.

TODAY
**I'll support a program at my school
that matters to me.**

September 19

"Put up a good front by sitting up front."
Randall McCutcheon

Randall McCutcheon is an award-winning teacher, so he knows what he's talking about when he advises students to sit up front. That's where the bright students usually sit if given the choice. They want to be near the action. When you sit up front, you're less likely to fall asleep in class. The teacher is more likely to notice you and get to know you. The class is more interesting, you're more involved, you're less likely to get distracted, and your self-confidence rises.

TODAY
If I can, I'll sit closer to the front of the class.

September 20

*"No snowflake in an avalanche
ever feels responsible."*
Stanislaus Lezczynski

"Everybody did it." "I didn't start it." "I was
just going along with the crowd." Sound famil-
iar? That kind of thinking has led to a lot of
silly fads and unspeakable horrors—lynchings,
hate crimes, the Holocaust, massacres in
Rwanda, ethnic cleansing in Kosovo.
Sociologist Robert Park called it "collective
behavior"—what happens when individuals
fall under the influence of an impulse that
results from social interaction. Others call it
mob rule. Everyone's involved, no one's responsible. Like snowflakes in an avalanche.

TODADY
**I'll think for myself
and make my own decisions.**

POSITIVE VALUES
ASSET #30: RESPONSIBILITY

September 21

"If you want to be a winner,
hang around with winners."
Christopher D. Furman

One of the best things you can do for yourself is to get a mentor—a caring adult who's willing to act as a guide and counselor to you. Adult mentors tend to be winners. They're successful in life and have a lot to share: wisdom, experience, insight, know-how. Many organizations and programs exist to make mentoring happen. Ask your school counselor for leads, or check with your local YMCA/YWCA or Junior Achievement. On the Web, visit the National Mentoring Partnership (www.mentoring.org) for tips on how to find a mentor.

TODAY
**I'll take the first step
toward getting a mentor.**

September 22

*"Peace is achieved one person at a time,
through a series of friendships."*
Fatma Reda

In 1994, a 15-year-old student named Shaun Proctor was shot and killed. In the aftermath of his death, his friends founded S.A.V.E.— Students Against Violence Everywhere. Today there are student-led S.A.V.E. programs in schools across the U.S. Sponsored by Mothers Against Violence in America (MAVIA), S.A.V.E. is open to all students who want to change attitudes and behaviors which contribute to violence. You might join (or start) a S.A.V.E. chapter in your school. Find out more at the MAVIA Web site (www.mavia.org).

TODAY
**I'll work for peace in my school
and community.**

September 23

> "I really do believe that we can all
> become better than we are."
> *James Baldwin*

Set high expectations for yourself. Share them with adults you trust. Ask for their encouragement. If the adults in your life don't have high expectations of you—if they respond to your hopes and dreams with indifference, put-downs, or criticism—then find adults who will give you the support you need. Many kids and teens meet caring adult mentors through youth organizations such as Big Brothers Big Sisters of America (www.bbbsa.org) and the Boys & Girls Clubs of America (www.bgca.org). See what's available in your community.

TODAY
**I'll talk with adults who expect good things
from me. Or I'll start looking
for adults who will.**

September 24

"I'm not an American hero.
I'm a person who loves children."
Clara McBride Hale

Clara McBride Hale, known as Mother Hale, overcame enormous difficulties in her own life, then founded the first facility in America dedicated to caring for babies born to drug-addicted mothers. In 1985, President Reagan cited her as an American hero. Are there people in your community who are known for helping kids? You might thank them for the good work they're doing. Is there a teacher, a coach, or a neighbor who makes you feel valued and appreciated? You might thank that person, too.

TODAY
**I'll notice and thank adults
who are helping kids and teens.**

EMPOWERMENT
ASSET #7: COMMUNITY VALUES YOUTH

September 25

"The reward of one duty is the power
to fulfill another."
George Eliot

Imagine you have a big science report that's due
in two weeks. (Or maybe you don't have to
imagine because it's true.) You've broken it
down into steps and made a list of what you
need to do and when. Today you finished the
first step. Now you can move on to the next—
and then the next, and the next after that.
You're confident that you'll complete your
report on time. Feels good, doesn't it?

TODAY
**I'll enjoy the satisfaction of working
toward a goal.**

September 26

"The only thing better than education
is more education."
Agnes Benedict

In a nationwide survey of 12,700 parents, 98 percent said they expect their children to graduate from high school. 88 percent said they expect them to attend college. 74 percent said they expect their kids to earn college degrees. What do your parents want for you? College? Grad school? An M.D. or law degree? Talk with your parents about their expectations. See if they agree with yours. Decide together how to proceed. It's not too soon to start thinking about, talking about, and planning your future education, if that's the direction you want to go.

TODAY
**I'll talk with my parents
about my future education.**

BOUNDARIES AND EXPECTATIONS
ASSET #16: HIGH EXPECTATIONS

September 27

"Sometimes you're the windshield,
sometimes you're the bug."
Mark Knopfler

Sometimes things go your way, sometimes they
don't. Sometimes you get what you want, sometimes you lose. But no matter what happens on
good days or bad, you always have personal
power. You are responsible for the kind of person you are and how you live your life. You are
responsible for your own behavior and feelings,
and you can make choices about them. No one
can tell you how to think or what to believe.
You can't control what other people do or
think, but why would you want to?

TODAY
I'll feel powerful.

POSITIVE IDENTITY
ASSET #37: PERSONAL POWER

September 28

"Please accept my resignation.
I don't care to belong to any club
that will have me as a member."
Groucho Marx

Groucho Marx wrote these famous words in a
letter to the Hollywood Friar's Club. He was a
comedian. It was his job to be funny. But
seriously...there are many clubs that would
welcome you as a member. Look around your
school and community. On the Web, go to
the National Youth Development Information Center site (www.nydic.org). Click on
"Directories" to find the *Directory of American
Youth Organizations* (www.nydic.org/dayo.
html). Then check out a searchable, up-to-date
listing of more than 500 national organizations
serving millions of American children and teens.

TODAY
I'll learn about clubs I might want to join.

CONSTRUCTIVE USE OF TIME
ASSET #18: YOUTH PROGRAMS

September 29

"Example is not the main thing
in influencing others. It is the only thing."
Albert Schweitzer

In one California high school, a group of 12th
graders formed a group to promote respect for
school boundaries. They explained the do's and
dont's of behavior to new students, and they
talked with students teachers were struggling
with. Grades and attendance improved, and
fewer new students spent time in the principal's
office. Alone or with your friends, you can be a
positive influence on other students. Especially
if you're a student leader, it's your job to follow
school rules. And even if you're not a leader,
you can act like one.

TODAY
**I'll be a positive role model for others
at my school.**

September 30

"A good education is the next best thing
to a pushy mother."
Charles Schulz

And sometimes it takes a pushy mother (or
father, or both) to make sure that you get the
best education possible. The more your parents
are involved in your schooling, the better it is
for you. Most parents are very active when
their kids are younger, then taper off during the
middle-school and high-school years. Some
parents get too busy to attend school conferences and events. Others believe their kids want
them to stay away. Tell your parents that you
want them to be involved. You need their
advice and support. If they are involved, let
them know how much you appreciate it.

TODAY
**I'll let my parents know that I want them
to be involved in my schooling.**

Support
Asset #6: Parent Involvement in Schooling

October 1

"The cure for boredom is curiosity."
Ellen Parr

According to Roper Starch Worldwide, a marketing, public opinion, advertising, and media research firm, "Curiosity may have killed the cat in the children's nursery rhyme. But in the current economy, it seems to be one of the keys to getting ahead." Curiosity keeps you interested and alert. It motivates you to ask questions and chase after answers. The more curious you are, the more new things you'll want to learn, and the more meaningful school will be.

TODAY
I'll be curious.

October 2

"We have the Bill of Rights. What we need is a Bill of Responsibilities."
Bill Maher

Try writing your own Bill of Responsibilities. Start by thinking of those you may have been neglecting—chores, homework, cleaning your room, holding up your end of a friendship. Consider ways to be more responsible for meeting your own needs. (What are some things your parents do for you that you could handle on your own?) Talk with your parents about what might happen if you behave more responsibly. Will you earn more privileges? More freedom to make your own decisions?

TODAY
I'll think about ways to be more responsible.

POSITIVE VALUES
ASSET #30: RESPONSIBILITY

October 3

"I am of the opinion that my life belongs
to the community...and as long as I live, it is
my privilege to do for it whatever I can."
George Bernard Shaw

What can you do for your community? Chris
Bergstrom was just 18 when he ran for City
Council in his hometown of Tualatin,
Oregon—and won. Jason Nastke was 19 when
he was elected mayor of Valatie, New York. If
running for office is too much for you, what
about campaigning for a candidate you believe
in? Or volunteering to work in the campaign
office? At the very least, you can vote when you
turn 18. According to surveys, most 18- to 24-
year-olds don't even bother to vote.

TODAY
**I'll consider becoming politically active
in my community.**

EMPOWERMENT
ASSET #8: YOUTH AS RESOURCES

277

October 4

"A good deed will make a good neighbor."
Bantu proverb

Find ways to serve your neighborhood. You can do this on your own, with your friends, or with your family. Start by thinking about individual neighbors or families who could use a hand. Don't forget seniors or singles. Can you weed a garden, shovel snow, paint a fence, or donate a few hours of baby-sitting time? Then think about your neighborhood as a whole. Is there a park that needs work? Graffiti that needs cleaning up or painting over? A vacant lot that could be turned into a neighborhood garden?

TODAY
I'll help a neighbor.

SUPPORT
ASSET #4: CARING NEIGHBORHOOD

October 5

"Students don't need condescending
cheerleading in 'self-esteem.'"
Camille Paglia

Professor, author, and self-proclaimed "dissident feminist" Camille Paglia is right. You don't need people telling you how wonderful you are. But you do need self-esteem. When you have self-esteem, you're more likely to take positive risks, accept responsibility for your actions, cope with life's changes and challenges, and bounce back from rejection, disappointment, failure, and defeat. Self-esteem isn't about being stuck-up or superior. It's not about compliments or flattery. It's about knowing yourself, being proud of yourself, and experiencing that pride from within.

TODAY
**I'll know that self-esteem comes
from the inside.**

POSITIVE IDENTITY
ASSET #38: SELF-ESTEEM

October 6

"Schools, by their very nature,
are breeding grounds for rudeness."
Alex J. Packer

Maybe your school rules and boundaries don't cover good manners. Maybe they should. Wouldn't it be great if people said "Please," "Thank you," "Excuse me," and "I'm sorry"? If they treated each other with kindness and respect? If they came to class prepared? If they didn't interrupt when others were talking? If they raised their hands? If they cleaned up after themselves? If they didn't use nasty language? If they did use deodorant and breath mints? In the words of Chinese philosopher Lao-Tzu, "The journey of a thousand miles begins with a single step."

TODAY
I'll be more polite in school.

October 7

"If you can't be a good example,
then you'll just have to be a horrible warning."
Catherine Aird

Influence is a two-way street. Your friends influence you, and you influence them. Are you a good example? A good leader? Are you someone who can be trusted? A person of good character—meaning someone who's honest, sincere, loyal, respectful, responsible? Are you serious about school? Do you have compassion? Do you stay out of trouble? Think about the kind of person you'd most like to have for a friend. Are you that kind of person yourself?

TODAY
I'll try to set a good example.

October 8

"When I was a kid my parents moved a lot, but I always found them."
Rodney Dangerfield

If your parents aren't involved in your schooling for whatever reason, let them know that you really want them to be involved. Then make it as easy for them as you can. Tell them about upcoming conferences and school events as soon as you know about them. Offer to write them on the family calendar. Give gentle reminders if you need to ("Mom, Dad, the game is tomorrow night—can you make it?"). When your teachers send home notes, schedules, and announcements, pass them on to your parents right away.

TODAY
I'll make sure my parents know about school events.

SUPPORT
ASSET #6: PARENT INVOLVEMENT IN SCHOOLING

October 9

"To give without any reward, or any notice,
has a special quality of its own."
Anne Morrow Lindbergh

It's nice if people notice when you're helpful.
It's great to get an award for a service project.
But try this today: Do a "secret service." Take
out the trash without being asked. Leave a treat
in a friend's locker or on a teacher's desk. Pick
up litter in a neighborhood park. Tuck a cheery
card into someone's backpack. Take a bag of
(clean, useful) clothes to a Salvation Army drop
box. Put a vase of flowers or a potted plant in
front of someone's door. Whatever you do,
don't tell anyone. Keep it to yourself. See how
it feels.

TODAY
I'll do a "secret service."

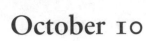

October 10

"If you deliberately plan on being less than you are capable of being, then I warn you that you'll be unhappy for the rest of your life."

Abraham Maslow

Some people always choose the easy way. Maybe they're lazy, maybe they're afraid, maybe they think it doesn't matter. When you don't push yourself, you plan for mediocrity. Right now is a great time to take risks and find out what you're made of. You probably don't have to support yourself, and you don't have as many responsibilities as you will when you're on your own. So imagine what you're capable of, then do it—or at least try. The world is full of frustrated people leading dull, boring lives. You don't have to be one of them.

TODAY
I'll challenge myself.

October 11

"It is not only for what we do that we
are held responsible, but also for what
we do not do."

Jean Baptiste Poquelin Molière

Are you a person who honors your commitments? If you say you'll be there at 8:00, do you show up late or not at all? If it's your night to cook dinner, do you forget or make other plans? If you don't do something you should, do you get defensive or blame someone else? When you honor your commitments, people learn to count on you. Friends trust you more. Adults (parents, teachers, coaches) reward you with more privileges and freedom. You feel stronger, more capable, more grown-up. You start to believe you have the power to shape your own life—and it's true.

TODAY
I'll honor a commitment.

October 12

"Are you a citizen? Act like one!"
MTV's ChooseorLose.com

MTV's ChooseorLose.com encourages political activism among younger voters. If you're not old enough to vote, you can still get involved in politics. Help campaign for a candidate you support. Join a youth organization like the Young Democrats or the Teen Age Republicans (or the Sub-Teen Age Republicans, called STARS). Keep up with local, state, and national politics by reading the newspaper and surfing newsy Web sites (CNN.com, Voter.com). You might even consider becoming a candidate yourself. Other teens have run—and won.

TODAY
I'll take the first step toward getting politically active.

CONSTRUCTIVE USE OF TIME
ASSET #18: YOUTH PROGRAMS

October 13

"Homework is something
that's got to be done."
Monica

If teen singing star Monica can do her homework, you can do yours. You may think that
young celebrities are exempt from such responsibilities. They're not. They go to school or, if
they're on movie or TV sets, study with tutors.
A few drop out to pursue their careers, but
most don't. And many go on to college. They're
famous, they're wealthy, and they know that's
not enough—they also want an education.

TODAY
I'll do my homework.

October 14

"In violence, we forget who we are."
Mary McCarthy

Did you really hit your brother? Was that you who called your best friend an awful name? Or got into a shoving match at school? Or smacked your girlfriend around? Or became so angry at the rude store clerk that you wished you could get her fired? Rage is a hot, red wind that changes us into people we don't want to know. We do things we could never imagine doing during quieter, saner moments. We hurt other people, sometimes in ways we can't ever fix. If you have a problem with anger and rage, get help.

TODAY
I'll learn positive ways to deal with anger and rage.

SOCIAL COMPETENCIES
ASSET #36: PEACEFUL CONFLICT RESOLUTION

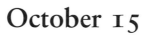

October 15

"My mother never gave up on me.
I messed up in school so much they were sending
me home, but my mother sent me right back."
Denzel Washington

If your parents are involved in your schooling—if they go to conferences and school events, if they ask about your day and care about how you do and offer to help with projects—you're lucky. Studies have shown that kids with involved parents are less likely to have learning and behavior problems, more likely to get higher grades and test scores, and more likely to go on to college. Studies have also shown that a lot of parents—up to 25 percent—don't really care about how their children are doing in school.

TODAY
I'll thank my parents for being involved in my schooling.

October 16

"The highest result of education
is tolerance."
Helen Keller

In a nationwide survey, public school students
in grades 7–12 were asked what they think
about multicultural education. 71 percent said
they were either very interested or somewhat
interested in learning more about other cultures. What are you learning in your school? A
little? A lot? You might become an advocate for
multicultural education. Talk with your teachers, your principal, the student council. When
you have a choice of projects to do in a class,
opt for one that broadens your knowledge of
other cultures.

TODAY
**I'll work for more multicultural education
at school.**

SOCIAL COMPETENCIES
ASSET #34: CULTURAL COMPETENCE

October 17

> "In the future, everyone will be famous
> for fifteen minutes."
> *Andy Warhol*

Children and teens who serve their communities deserve their 15 minutes of fame. There are many local and national organizations that honor kids with awards and recognition. (Some give certificates and pins, others give cash awards and scholarships.) Is there someone you know who works hard to help other people in your community or beyond? Is he or she going unnoticed? Tell an adult (a teacher, youth leader, coach, or someone else who cares) about that person.

TODAY
**I'll call attention to a child or teen
who deserves to be noticed.**

October 18

"No act of kindness, no matter how small,
is ever wasted."
Aesop

If you want your school to be a more caring place, then be more caring yourself. Learn the names of as many students as you can. Smile and say hi when you see them in the halls, in the cafeteria, at games. Be nice to kids who seem isolated or lonely. Stick up for kids who are bullied or teased. If your school has a peer helping program, get involved.

TODAY
I'll reach out to someone at school.

October 19

"There is no more beautiful life
than that of a student."

F. Albrecht

Maybe you wish you didn't have to go to
school. Or there are days when you stare out
the window and think, "I'd rather be anywhere
than here." If you lived in a developing country,
you might be one of the 250 million children
ages 5–14 who'd give anything to be in school.
Instead, they're working, often under forced
labor conditions and in bondage. By the way,
this 250 million figure is an estimate, and it
doesn't include the millions more who are
unpaid workers in their parents' or guardians'
homes. Would you trade places?

TODAY
I'll be glad I'm in school.

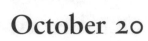

October 20

"I never got an A in more than one class in a semester. But I loved reading nonfiction because it made me feel smart."

Tom Hanks

The next time you're looking for something to read, head for the nonfiction section of the library or bookstore. Find a book or two about traveling through Borneo, or growing up in ancient Rome, or climbing Mt. Everest, or painting a landscape, or building a sailboat, or designing cars, or training dogs, or whatever else interests you even a little. Maybe the only nonfiction you've read so far is in textbooks. There's a lot more out there, and some of it is great reading.

TODAY
I'll read some nonfiction.

October 21

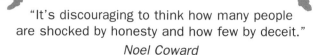

"It's discouraging to think how many people are shocked by honesty and how few by deceit."
Noel Coward

Lying has become commonplace. We expect politicians to fudge the truth. We're not surprised when business people are less than honest. Half-truths, white lies, distortions, rationalizations, exaggerations, excuses, fibs... is there a difference? Does it matter? Is it always better to tell the truth? Is it sometimes better to lie if it keeps us out of trouble or saves someone else's feelings? Is it okay to lie if we know we won't get caught? It's so confusing! No wonder that according to a recent Gallup Youth Survey, 96 percent of teens believe that lessons in honesty should be part of the school curriculum.

TODAY
I'll think about what it means to be honest.

POSITIVE VALUES
ASSET #29: HONESTY

October 22

"Failing to prepare is preparing to fail."
John Wooden

What would you do if you were at a party and saw someone with a gun? If you got in a friend's car and realized the driver was drunk? If your date was pressuring you for sex and wouldn't take no for an answer? What if you were at a club and a stranger handed you a drink? When you're scared and confused is no time to be figuring things out. You need to know in advance how to stay safe. Talk with your parents. Talk with your friends (and agree to watch out for each other). Ask your teachers if you can spend class time role-playing situations like these.

TODAY
I'll plan ahead for dangerous times.

October 23

"We're just a group of dads who want
to get involved and help save our children."
Tommy Stout

At high schools in Indianapolis, Indiana, and
Baton Rouge, Louisiana, fathers like Tommy
Stout walk the halls, monitor the cafeteria and
library, attend school events (games, dances,
concerts), act as peacekeepers and role models,
and listen to kids who need someone to talk to.
They wear shirts and hats with "Security Dad"
logos so they're easy to recognize. The schools
feel safer, and students show more respect for
their schools and adults.

TODAY
I'll think of ways to get parents more involved at my school.

October 24

"If our shirttails aren't tucked in,
  we get a detention!"
Posting on a teen message board

You've heard kids complain about school rules.
Would it surprise you to learn that some students wish their schools had tougher rules? In
one survey of over 1,300 high school students,
79 percent said they would learn more if
schools enforced being on time and completing
homework. In a survey of more than 218,000
students in grades 6–12, 58 percent said that
school officials should be able to search students' lockers for drugs or weapons without
permission. 75 percent think schools should
ban clothing with gang symbols. And 69 percent say students should be required to stand
during the national anthem.

TODAY
**I'll work for stronger rules at my school,
if that's what I think it needs.**

BOUNDARIES AND EXPECTATIONS
ASSET #12: SCHOOL BOUNDARIES

October 25

"A community is like a ship. Everyone
ought to be prepared to take the helm."
Henrik Ibsen

Who's watching out for younger kids in your
neighborhood? Are there some who seem to be
heading for trouble? Maybe they're unsuper-
vised for long periods of time. Maybe they don't
have anything better to do. If you want, you can
be a positive influence. Learn their names. Say
hi when you see them. Talk to them. Show an
interest in them. When you notice behavior
that's out of bounds, call them on it. You might
start a club for neighborhood kids. Or be a telephone friend for a latchkey kid.

TODAY
**I'll keep an eye on younger kids in my
neighborhood.**

October 26

"Life is 10 percent what you make it and 90 percent how you take it."
Irving Berlin

Don't like school? Try a new attitude. Even in the class you like the least, you can probably find one thing that sparks your interest. Relate what you're learning to real life. Resist all urges to doze off or daydream. Do the homework. Participate in class discussions; ask questions about things you don't understand. See if your teacher will let you do papers, projects, and reports on topics you choose instead of the standard assignments. Make an effort to be part of the class and you'll notice a difference in how you feel about it. Your teacher will notice, too. Teachers appreciate enthusiastic students.

TODAY
I'll have a positive attitude about school.

COMMITMENT TO LEARNING
ASSET #22: SCHOOL ENGAGEMENT

October 27

*"Leisure is the time
for doing something useful."*
Benjamin Franklin

Got time on your hands? Maybe it doesn't seem that way to you, with school and chores and friends and sports and clubs and other commitments. Or maybe you spend most of your life on the computer, on the phone, or in front of the TV. How much time are you wasting on things that don't really matter? Think about spending one hour each day helping someone, somewhere—around the house, in your neighborhood, at school, in the community. Your life will be more meaningful and your self-esteem will soar.

TODAY
I'll spend an hour doing something useful.

October 28

"Education is too important to be left
solely to the educators."

Francis Keppel

Parent involvement in schooling is so important
that in 1994 the Governors and Congress of the
United States made it one of the eight National
Education Goals. Schools are supposed to
"promote partnerships that will increase
parental involvement and participation in pro-
moting the social, emotional, and academic
growth of children." Are parents welcome at
your school? Are they encouraged to get
involved? Find out what your school is doing to
"promote partnerships" with parents. If you
don't think they're doing enough, or you have
other ideas, offer to help.

TODAY

**I'll find out what my school is doing
to get and keep parents involved.**

October 29

"Look for your choices,
pick the best one, then go with it."
Pat Riley

Have you explored all of the options available
to you at school? Like special classes, opportunities for independent study, apprenticeships,
mini-courses, tutoring (if you need it), AP
classes, enrichment programs, even college
courses? (In some states, you can take college-
level classes while you're still in high school,
and the state will pay your tuition.) If you're
not thrilled about school, or if you want to
make the most of your years in school, know
what's out there. Talk with the school counselor to learn what's right for you.

TODAY
I'll explore my options at school.

October 30

"Peace—that was the other name for home."
Kathleen Norris

Maybe your other name for home is World War III. Maybe it doesn't have to be that way, and if it weren't, maybe everyone would enjoy it more, including you. Is it time to call a truce on at least one of your endless battles with your parents? About hair or curfew or friends or attitude or language or clothes or school or the fact that all of the CDs you buy come with advisory stickers? What if you try talking with your parents and make an effort to see their side? It can't hurt and it might cut down on some of the arguing.

TODAY
I'll do my part to make my home more peaceful.

CONSTRUCTIVE USE OF TIME
ASSET #20: TIME AT HOME

October 31

"Misery loves company."
Anonymous

If you really hate homework, this might help: Start a study group. It's less lonely and more fun than studying alone. Keep it small—three or four people max. Meet frequently for shorter sessions instead of rarely for marathons. Follow an agenda and hold everyone responsible for being prepared and making a contribution. Words to the wise from teacher and author Randall McCutcheon: "Do not form a 'study group' unless you plan to study." Otherwise it's a waste of time and you'll end up doing your homework alone anyway.

TODAY
I'll make a list of people I might want to study with.

November 1

"That's what being young is all about.
You have the courage and the daring
to think that you can make a difference."
Ruby Dee

You can't fight crime and make your community safer—or can you? Check with your local police to learn if there's a crimefighting program for youth in your area. If you want, you can get involved with a national program. See if Teens, Crime, and the Community (www.national tcc.org) has a site near you. Join or start a Youth Crime Watch program (www.ycwa.org).

TODAY
I'll learn about ways to fight crime in my community.

306

November 2

"People deserve...the truth.
They deserve honesty."
Bruce Springsteen

Designer labels won't make you popular. Breath mints won't make you strong. Potato chips won't make you sexy. No matter what advertisements claim. All those promises have one purpose: getting between you and your money. What's more important? You decide. Want to know more about advertising? Check out *Adbusters*, a quarterly magazine for people who are tired of TV and magazine ads full of stereotypes, sexism, and propaganda. See if your library subscribes, or visit the Web site (www.adbusters.org).

TODAY
I won't believe the hype.

November 3

"America has become numb to violence
because it just drowns in it, day in and day out."
Janet Reno

According to the American Psychological
Association, the average 12-year-old has seen
8,000 murders and 100,000 acts of violence on
network television. Shootings, assaults with
other weapons, beatings, suicides, sexual
assaults, brawls, and blood-spattered walls are
our nightly entertainment. More than 80 percent of Americans believe TV violence is harm-
ful. The American Medical Association has
passed a resolution declaring that TV violence
"threatens the health and welfare of young
Americans." Why are you watching?

TODAY
I'll take the day off from violent TV programs.

November 4

"Success in life is a matter not so much of talent as of concentration and perseverance."
C.W. Wendte

Concentration and perseverance are two things that homework can teach you. They're skills you need to succeed in school and at almost any job you do or career you pursue. So try not to hate homework too much. Find a quiet, comfortable, well-lit place to do it. If you think your study skills could use improvement, get help. Ask your teacher for suggestions. Or ask the media specialist at your school to recommend a book or cassette.

TODAY
I'll be serious about homework.

November 5

"I think a hero is an ordinary individual
who finds strength to persevere and endure
in spite of overwhelming obstacles."
Christopher Reeve

From his movie roles, the world knew him as Superman—man of steel. Then, in May 1995, Christopher Reeve fell from his horse during a riding show competition and was paralyzed from the neck down. He could have become a recluse. Instead, he became a vocal proponent for people with disabilities (especially those with spinal cord injuries), speaking out before Congress and wherever people would listen. Reeve used to define a hero as "someone who commits a courageous action without considering the consequences." Experience changed his definition.

TODAY
I'll come up with my own definition of a hero.

BOUNDARIES AND EXPECTATIONS
ASSET #14: ADULT ROLE MODELS

November 6

"It is not who you attend school with but who controls the school you attend."
Nikki Giovanni

School starts to feel a lot different when you get to know a teacher. Or have a good talk with your principal. Or make friends with a secretary or custodian. Or volunteer to help in the media center after school. This isn't kissing up; it's being smart. It's getting connected in ways that don't occur to a lot of teens. It's going beyond your circle of same-age, same-interests friends. Suddenly teachers and administrators are more than a faceless bunch of adults. They're people you say hi to and smile at in the halls.

TODAY
I'll connect with an adult at my school.

SUPPORT
ASSET #5: CARING SCHOOL CLIMATE

November 7

"In a democracy, the individual enjoys
not only the ultimate power but carries
the ultimate responsibility."

Norman Cousins

Fewer than 1 in 3 young adults ages 18–24 voted in the 1996 U.S. presidential election. Nearly 2 out of 3 seniors ages 65–74 voted. No wonder politicians don't seem to care what young people think. Why focus on people who don't or won't vote? Promise yourself that as soon as you turn 18, you'll register to vote. Promise that you'll vote in every election, including primaries. P.S. There are a *lot* more 18- to 24-year-olds in the U.S. today than 65- to 74-year-olds. If 2 out of 3 young adults voted, they would control the elections.

TODAY
**I'll learn how to register to vote
in my county or state.**

November 8

"The nice thing about teamwork is
that you always have others on your side."
Margaret Carty

Having problems at school? Not sure how to
solve them on your own? Get your parents on
your team. Tell them what's happening and ask
for their help. If your problems are in a particular class, meet and talk with the teacher. Not
you and the teacher, or your parents and the
teacher, but you *and* your parents and the
teacher.

TODAY
**I'll ask my parents for help
with a school problem.**

November 9

"The purpose of education is to replace
an empty mind with an open one."
Malcolm Forbes

Be open to the possibilities available at your
school. To meet new people. To learn new
things. To challenge yourself in ways you never
imagined. To form a close and lasting relationship with a teacher. (Some people stay in touch
with their teachers for years.) To try out for a
team. To join a club or two. To discover that
you don't hate math after all. To run for student
council. To write for the school newspaper. To
peer into a microscope and see amazing things.
What else?

TODAY
I'll keep an open mind about school.

November 10

"Rules are made for people who aren't willing to make up their own."
Chuck Yeager

If everyone came to school on time, there wouldn't be any tardiness rules. If no one brought guns or knives to school, there wouldn't be any weapons rules. If cheating and plagiarism weren't problems, there wouldn't be rules about them. And so on. Most school rules exist because sometime, somewhere, someone made them necessary. The more responsible you are, the less you'll need to worry about rules because you won't be breaking them.

TODAY
I'll behave responsibly at school.

November 11

*"All of us, at certain moments of our lives,
need to take advice and receive help
from other people."*
Alexis Carrel

When you belong to a religious community,
you have plenty of people you can ask for
advice about your values and beliefs—the core
of who you are. Many schools and organizations shy away from teaching values. Your religious community may be the only place you
spend time (outside your family) where people
talk openly about values. You need adults in
your life who aren't afraid to say "This is right"
or "That's wrong"—even if you don't always
agree with them.

TODAY
**I'll ask a religious leader for advice
on something I'm struggling with.**

CONSTRUCTIVE USE OF TIME
ASSET #19: RELIGIOUS COMMUNITY

November 12

"It is possible to be different
and still be all right."
Anne Wilson Schaef

You don't have to be, look, think, act, dress, believe, and/or feel like everyone else. Or even like one other person you know or admire or envy. Why would you want to? It's your job, your assignment in life, your lucky break to be unique, different, and one of a kind. Dr. Sol Gordon, a respected educator and author, once wrote, "There will always be people who appear to be handsomer, prettier, richer, luckier, and better-educated than you. What's the point of comparing? We are all created equal. We are all created to serve in a special way."

TODAY
I'll be myself.

November 13

"If at first you don't succeed, cheat!"
Graffiti

Students and teachers alike say that cheating is
a big problem in schools today. When 3,200
high-achieving high school students were asked
about cheating, 88 percent said that cheating
was widespread in their school. 76 percent
admitted they had cheated on their school
work; 38 percent said they had cheated on a
test or quiz. 60 percent of those who cheated
said "it didn't seem like a big deal." In another
survey of 356 high school teachers, 9 out of 10
said that cheating was a problem, and half said
they encountered students cheating in most of
their classes.

TODAY
**I'll learn about the consequences
of cheating at my school.**

POSITIVE VALUES
ASSET #29: HONESTY

November 14

"It's nice to be important,
but it's more important to be nice."
John Cassis

Even to your friends. Especially to your friends. In the words of manners guru Alex J. Packer, author of *How Rude! The Teenagers' Guide to Good Manners, Proper Behavior, and Not Grossing People Out,* "Teenagers who practice good manners with their peers can dodge much of the suffering and anxiety that runs rampant in school corridors. And they will enjoy closer and more rewarding relationships with their friends and romantic interests." Try treating your friends politely and see what a difference it makes.

TODAY
I'll be polite to my friends.

November 15

"You must get involved to have an impact.
No one is impressed with the won-lost
record of the referee."

John H. Holcomb

Is there something about your school you
absolutely hate? Don't just whine about it. Do
something to make it better. Run for student
council or join another leadership organization.
Start a campaign, take a survey, form a committee, come up with a plan. Maybe there's an
old school rule that needs changing. Maybe
there's too much litter in the halls. Maybe you
think after-school tutoring should be available
for students who need it. What's your idea?

TODAY
**I'll work to change something at my school
that needs changing.**

November 16

"The more you study, the more you
find out you don't know, but the more you
study, the closer you come."
Cozy Cole

You look at your homework—that gross, dis-
gusting pile of books and papers—and you may
want to throw up. Your first impulse is to reach
for the easiest assignment. Something you can
actually bear to do. Something you can breeze
through without a lot of effort. Try this instead:
Take a minute to prioritize your homework.
Then do the hardest assignment first. Why?
Because you're fresher when you start than you
will be in an hour or two. You'll have the satisfaction of getting the worst part out of the way.
And everything else will be easier.

TODAY
I'll do my hardest homework first.

COMMITMENT TO LEARNING
ASSET #23: HOMEWORK

November 17

"The word 'don't' in anything doesn't work.
It makes you want to do the opposite."
April Kaeder

Too bad there's not another word for "don't,"
because teens are sick of it. Don't drink. Don't
smoke. Don't use drugs. Don't have sex, or at
least don't have unprotected sex. Don't go
there. Don't do that. And on and on, blah blah
blah. It's a word that goes along with a stern
face, a wagging finger, or that "please listen!"
look adults wear when they talk with you
about Big Important Things. Until someone
comes up with a different word, we're stuck
with "don't." Try seeing beyond it to the positive messages buried in there somewhere: Be
safe. Be healthy. Be smart. Stay alive.

TODAY
**I'll be open to good advice, even if it comes
with a "don't."**

November 18

"Teaching is not a lost art, but the regard
for it is a lost tradition."

Jacques Barzun

You've heard that teachers are underpaid, and maybe you've thought, "Yeah, right." In fact, experienced teachers with masters' degrees earn about $32,000 less per year than other college graduates. Plus teaching is getting tougher every year. Classrooms are crowded, resources are shrinking, working conditions are poor, students are rude, and growing immigrant populations are challenging (how do you teach a class where many students don't speak English?). So give your teachers a break.

TODAY
I'll appreciate my teachers.

November 19

"Bias has to be taught. If you hear your
parents downgrading women or people
of different backgrounds, why,
you are going to do that."

Barbara Bush

Even if you grow up hearing that certain people
and races are inferior—from your parents,
grandparents, or other adults—you don't have
to accept their beliefs as your own. You can
choose to learn, explore, experience, and decide
for yourself that you won't let prejudice shape
your life. Get to know people of different races
and backgrounds at school and in your community. Join a club, team, or youth group with
a diverse membership. You owe it to yourself
and your future.

TODAY
**I won't let other people's prejudices
influence me.**

SOCIAL COMPETENCIES
ASSET #34: CULTURAL COMPETENCE

November 20

"Tact is the knack of making a point
without making an enemy."
Sir Isaac Newton

Honesty gets tricky when we know we can hurt someone's feelings by telling the truth. Which is better? To be honest anyway? To be sort of honest? To lie? Change the subject? Say nothing? In your own life, you'll have to judge this one encounter at a time. When telling the truth could be painful, ask yourself, "Who will this help?" If the answer is "no one" or "me, but only because I'll feel powerful," choose a kinder, gentler way. To the friend with the hideous haircut who asks, "What do you think?" you might say, "It's unique. Just like you."

TODAY
I'll be tactful.

November 21

"I believe that as a role model I have
the responsibility to let young people know that
you can make a mistake and come back from it."
Ann Richards

In 1982, Ann Richards was elected treasurer of
Texas, the first woman to hold a state office
there in 50 years. She defeated her opponent
after an ugly campaign that focused on a problem Richards had: She was an alcoholic who
had gone through treatment. Instead of avoid-
ing the issue, Richards was up front and honest
about it. She was reelected in 1986, and in
1990 she ran for governor and won. Today she
is widely admired for her independence, open-
ness, courage, and wit.

TODAY
**I'll look for a role model who has learned
from a mistake.**

BOUNDARIES AND EXPECTATIONS
ASSET #14: ADULT ROLE MODELS

November 22

"Your own safety is at stake
when your neighbor's wall is ablaze."
Horace

Don't close your eyes and ears to problems you
notice in your neighborhood. Even if they don't
affect you personally. Even if you think they're
none of your business. A dangerous intersec-
tion, graffiti across the alley, a broken lock on
an apartment doorway, an animal that's being
abused, a child who's being neglected, an elderly
person who lives alone and never has visitors,
suspicious activity on a street corner—what if
everyone pretends not to see? If you don't think
you can do anything on your own, or you're
afraid to get involved, talk to your parents or
other adults you trust.

TODAY
I won't ignore problems in my neighborhood.

November 23

> "It's easy to make a buck. It's a lot tougher to make a difference."
>
> *Tom Brokaw*

In a recent survey of more than 193,000 students in grades 6–12, 33 percent said money is very important when it comes to being happy. 19 percent expect to be earning $50,000 a year by the time they're 30; 17 percent expect to be earning more than $100,000. 52 percent think they'll be better off than their parents. It's good to aim for financial independence. You want to be able to support yourself. But try not to let money become what you live for. As Ralph Waldo Emerson once said, "Money often costs too much."

TODAY
I'll put money in perspective.

POSITIVE IDENTITY
ASSET #39: SENSE OF PURPOSE

November 24

"How do you explain school
to a higher intelligence?"
Elliot in E.T. the Extra-Terrestrial

When you talk about your school, what do you say? Good things? Bad things? Maybe it's cool to disrespect your school. But the things you say can affect the way you feel. The next time your friends get into a school-bashing session, stay neutral. Or mention one thing you like about school and see how it flies. Something like, "Come on, it's not that awful. At least the tacos at lunch today were edible."

TODAY
I'll talk positively about my school.

November 25

"Sometimes you gotta create
what you want to be a part of."
Geri Weitzman

Do you ever wish your family were closer?
Warmer? More caring? More interesting? More
fun? You'll spend 18 years of your life with
them, maybe longer. Why waste those years
counting the months and days and hours and
minutes until you can finally leave? If you want
more from your family, you might start by giving more. Show some interest in your parents
and siblings. Share some of yourself with
them—your interests, thoughts, activities, concerns, hopes and dreams. Instead of staying in
your room or going out with your friends,
make an effort to be with your family. See if
things improve.

TODAY
I'll work to bring my family closer.

CONSTRUCTIVE USE OF TIME
ASSET #20: TIME AT HOME

November 26

"Because I'm technologically able to find a like-minded person on the other side of the globe, I'm also more interested in making friends with my next-door neighbor."
Jeffrey Klein

We meet in chat rooms, on message boards, in online games. We communicate with email, instant messages, digital photos, video clips, and sound files. We make friends with people we never would have met without the Internet. Technology is making the world seem smaller every day. But there's still something special about face-to-face, in-person conversation. So even if you're having great online relationships with friends in Japan and Sweden (or whcrever), log off once in a while and have a chat with someone whose hand you can shake for real.

TODAY
I'll spend time with a neighbor.

November 27

"What's wrong with having school spirit? It's all about having fun. You're only in high school once, why not make the best of it?"

Posting on a teen message board

On the same message board, teens were invited to respond to the question, "Do you have school spirit?" 57 percent said yes. 43 percent said no. School spirit may be corny, but it does link students who might have little or nothing in common otherwise. And it makes school more bearable, even enjoyable. If your school spirit is weak or nonexistent, try building it up. Wear a school sweatshirt. Go to school events. Hang around with other kids who have school spirit. It won't hurt and it might help.

TODAY

I'll have school spirit.

November 28

*"What it lies in our power to do,
it lies in our power not to do."*
Aristotle

Your parents can talk, plead, and lecture. Your religious leaders can advise and sermonize. Your teachers, youth leaders, coaches, mentors, and other adults you know can give you their two cents, invited or not. But only you can make the ultimate decisions about what you will and won't do. You've got the power to say yes, no, not yet, maybe later, and sorry, that's not for me—not now, not ever, good-bye, get lost. The only person who can really stop you from doing something you shouldn't is you.

TODAY
I'll know my own power.

November 29

> "Heirlooms we don't have in our family.
> But stories we've got."
> *Rose Chernin*

It's fun to remember and share family stories. If you have favorites, you might want to write them down (or record them on tape or CD) so you don't forget them. The next time you add pictures to your family photo album, jot down notes about when and where the pictures were taken and anything special you don't want to forget. Is your family into reunions? Offer to help compile a newsletter or booklet of family stories. One family keeps a "Family Lore" notebook, with descriptions of happy and memorable times. Even sad stories are worth recording.

TODAY
I'll ask my parents to tell me a family story.

November 30

"Set your sights high—the higher
the better. Expect the most wonderful
things to happen.... Allow absolutely nothing
to hamper you or hold you up in any way."
Eileen Caddy

Other people may try to block your progress.
Don't let them. Instead, be a football player running for a touchdown. A heat-seeking missile. A
salmon swimming upstream. An eagle after its
prey. A raft running the rapids. A rocket at lift-
off. A cat in hot pursuit of a mouse. A dog in
hot pursuit of a cat. Be Marion Jones on her
way to an Olympic medal. Or Kevin Garnett on
his way to the hoop. Be Edmund Hillary and
Tenzing Norgay climbing Mt. Everest. Come up
with your own metaphor and let it inspire you.

TODAY
I won't let anything stand in my way.

December 1

*"The thing that makes a creative person
is to be creative and that is all there is to it."*
Edward Albee

Maybe you've always wanted to play the guitar.
Or sing in a chorus. Or act in a play. Or throw
a pot (that's make one, not break one). So
what's stopping you? No time? Take another
look at your schedule or the way you spend
your free time. No money? See if your school
offers classes, clubs, or after-school programs.
Check out classes offered through community
education and arts centers, the YMCA and
YWCA. Find a talented neighbor or relative
who's willing to teach you. Explore your
options. No more excuses.

TODAY
I'll be creative.

CONSTRUCTIVE USE OF TIME
ASSET #17: CREATIVE ACTIVITIES

December 2

"The only pressure I'm under is
the pressure I've put on myself."
Mark Messier

Who says you have to dress a certain way, act a
certain way, think a certain way, and only hang
out with certain people? One easy answer is
"My friends." BUZZ! Think again. Who's
pulling the clothes out of your closet? Putting
words in your mouth? Telling your feet to go
right instead of left? Whose brain is doing the
thinking? Peer pressure can be heavy and hard
to resist, but what you do is up to you.

TODAY
**I'll take responsibility for my thoughts
and actions.**

December 3

"Putting off tough jobs makes them harder."
Marva Collins

You've got a big assignment due, next week or next month or whenever. You can hardly stand to think about it—maybe it's in your worst subject or a class you can't stay awake in because it's soooo borrrrinnnng—so you've been procrastinating. Do yourself a favor. Start it today. The longer you wait, the more you'll dread it, until one day dread is replaced by panic because you've run out of time. Take the first step. Even if it's a baby step. Just getting started will make a difference in how you feel.

TODAY
**I'll work on an assignment
I've been putting off.**

COMMITMENT TO LEARNING
ASSET #23: HOMEWORK

December 4

"I never learn anything talking.
I only learn things when I ask questions."
Lou Holtz

Your parents were teenagers once (duh). They probably went through a lot of the same things you're going through right now. Don't believe it? Ask them. Ask about their good times and bad, their successes and frustrations. Ask what they're proudest of when they think back on their teenage years, and what they wish they could do over. You'll probably find that they've been there, done that, and their insights and experiences might help you get through a rough time.

TODAY
I'll ask questions.

December 5

"When your values are clear to you,
making decisions becomes easier."
Roy Disney

When teenagers who've never had sex are asked
why they abstain, what's the main reason they
give? It's not the desire to avoid pregnancy, the
fear of sexually transmitted diseases, or the fact
that they haven't met the right person. The main
reason is that having sex would go against their
religious or moral values. The stronger and
clearer your values are, the simpler it is to make
decisions—even tough decisions.

TODAY
I'll be sure I know what my values are.

POSITIVE VALUES
ASSET #31: RESTRAINT

December 6

"Humility is the ability to act embarrassed
when you tell people how wonderful you are."
S. Lee Buchansky

Bragging about yourself can keep a friendship
from starting. It can strain an old friendship to
the breaking point. It's okay to share good news
about your successes and achievements with
people you know, and your real friends will be
happy for you. But when you're meeting someone for the first time, and especially if you want
to impress him or her, try to find something to
talk about besides yourself.

TODAY
I won't brag about myself.

December 7

"There is nothing like staying home for real comfort."

Jane Austen

It's where your stuff is. There's (hopefully) food in the fridge. You can walk around with bad hair. People know you—your quirks, faults, and flaws—and they like you anyway. Why be in such a rush to get out the door? If it's a school day, plan to spend the evening at home. If it's a weekend, how about the whole day? Talk with your parents. Read to your little brother or sis. Clean your room. Play chase-the-string with the cat. Bake brownies. Do chores. Listen to music. Stretch out on the sofa and read old issues of *National Geographic*. Whatever.

TODAY
I'll stay home.

CONSTRUCTIVE USE OF TIME
ASSET #20: TIME AT HOME

December 8

"The most important thing that parents
can teach their children is how
to get along without them."
Frank A. Clark

Your parents have worried about you since you
were born. Someday they'd like to worry less.
They want to know you'll be okay on your
own, out in the world, without their protection
and financial support. If they're making rules
now (and grounding you when you break
them), that's part of their grand plan to help
you become independent. When you look at it
that way, rules don't seem so bad and limits
aren't so oppressive.

TODAY
**I'll know that my parents make rules
for a reason.**

Boundaries and Expectations
Asset #11: Family Boundaries

December 9

> "No greater challenge exists today
> than creating safe schools."
> *Ronald D. Stephens*

The executive director of the National School Safety Center, Ronald Stephens describes a safe school as a place where "students can learn and teachers can teach in a welcoming environment, free of intimidation and fear." It's a place where "behavior expectations are clearly communicated, consistently enforced, and fairly applied." If your school has boundaries, be glad. Some schools don't, and you wouldn't want to go there.

TODAY
I'll be glad that my school has boundaries.

December 10

"All human beings are born free and equal in dignity and rights."

From Article I of the Universal Declaration of Human Rights

On December 10, 1948, the General Assembly of the United Nations adopted and proclaimed the Universal Declaration of Human Rights. The UDHR describes 30 basic human rights that belong to everyone. You can read the complete text at your library or on the Web (for example, at www.un.org/overview/rights.html). If you want to go further, visit the Human Rights Watch Web site (www.hrw.org) and learn about an organization dedicated to protecting the human rights of people around the world. How can you get involved? What can you do?

TODAY
I'll learn more about human rights.

POSITIVE VALUES
ASSET #27: EQUALITY AND SOCIAL JUSTICE

December 11

"The truth is out there."
The X-Files

In your search for truth and honesty (and you are searching, right?), don't forget to look in the most obvious place: in there. Inside yourself. Are you someone who values honesty? Are you truthful with your parents, your siblings, other family members, friends, teachers, neighbors, coaches, strangers? When you're less than honest, do you admit it, apologize, and make things right? Have you made a personal commitment to being honest?

TODAY
I'll tell the truth—even when it's not easy.

POSITIVE VALUES
ASSET #29: HONESTY

December 12

"What is important is not that there are uncontrollable events in our lives, but how we respond to them."
Hyrum W. Smith

There are many things in your life you can't control. Which you probably already know. But that doesn't mean you're helpless or you lack personal power. How you respond to the things in your life is 100 percent your call. You can decide to be sad, mad, frustrated, glad, indifferent, or anything else you choose. No one can control what you think or feel. That's power.

TODAY
**I'll decide how to respond
to events in my life.**

POSITIVE IDENTITY
ASSET #37: PERSONAL POWER

December 13

*"There are high spots in all of our lives
and most of them have come about through
encouragement from someone else."*
George Matthew Adams

Does an adult you know trust you with an important job? Count on you to do something that matters? Rely on your skills and judgment? Maybe you're the one who's there when your younger siblings get home from school. Or your parents come to you to solve their computer problems. We feel valued when someone gives us useful, meaningful things to do. Sometimes it's a pain, but it's also good practice.

TODAY
I'll live up to my responsibilities.

December 14

"I find that a great part of the information
I have was acquired by looking up something
and finding something else on the way."
Franklin P. Adams

Have you ever gone looking for a particular
fact—in an encyclopedia, on the Web, in library
stacks—and gotten totally sucked in and car-
ried away? You need Orville Wright's birth
date, and suddenly it's hours later and you're
reading about monkeys of the upper Amazon.
University of Chicago professor Mihaly
Csikszentmihalyi calls this "flow." You're so
absorbed in what you're doing that you lose all
track of time. The experience of learning
becomes its own reward. The Web, with its zil-
lions of links, is perfect for inducing the flow
state. You never know where you'll end up, and
it's all about the journey.

TODAY
I'll go with the "flow."

COMMITMENT TO LEARNING
ASSET #25: READING FOR PLEASURE

December 15

"How can you have a family
if you don't have family dinner?"
Jane Cutler

Life is so hectic and everyone's so busy that
family dinner—everyone around the table,
sharing food and conversation—seems like an
impossible dream. It may take work to make it
happen, but it's worth it. Family dinner is one
of the best ways to build a strong family and
improve family communication. You might
take the lead in making family dinner (once a
week? twice a week? more?) a priority in your
home. Tell your parents this is something you
want and offer to help.

TODAY
I'll eat dinner with my family.

December 16

"Too many people grow up.... They don't
remember what it's like to be 12 years old.
They patronize, they treat children as inferiors."
Walt Disney

Think back on what it was like to be a kid. (If
you're 12 or younger, think back to when you
were 6 or 7.) Remember how it felt when people
treated you like an inferior, or acted as if your
opinion didn't matter, or assumed you didn't
know much because you were young. Now think
about how you treat kids who are younger than
you are today. Are you proud of your behavior,
or would you like to make a change?

TODAY
I'll treat younger kids with respect.

December 17

"I've been called nerd, geek, every name in the book. I really didn't let it faze me. I'm no nerd. I'm just a person who is very determined in this life."

Woodlyne Jean-Charles

Woodlyne's determination brought her a gold medal in the Afro-Academic, Cultural, Technological, and Scientific Olympics (ACT-SO), sponsored by the NAACP. She was 17 when she earned her medal. Other "nerds" and "geeks" had to wait a bit longer for fame and recognition. Like Steve Jobs, cofounder of Apple Computer. And Bill Gates, founder of Microsoft. And Jeff Bezos, founder of Amazon.com. Given the growing popularity of computers and the Internet, there's never been a better time to be a nerd. If you're one, go for it.

TODAY
I won't care if someone calls me names.

POSITIVE IDENTITY
ASSET #38: SELF-ESTEEM

December 18

"High expectations are the key
to everything."
Sam Walton

Who has high expectations for you? Who believes—really believes—that you can and will succeed in life? Maybe it's your grandmother. Maybe it's your mom or dad. Maybe it's a teacher who's known you since you were little and still stays in touch. Maybe it's a youth leader, or a favorite uncle or aunt. Whoever it is, that person is important to you. And if there's more than one person rooting for you, you're even luckier. When people we care about want us to do well, we try harder. We feel more capable and willing to take positive risks.

TODAY
**I'll be grateful for people in my life
who expect me to do well.**

December 19

"Who remembers what I said? I was a kid!"
Kirsten Dunst

In 1994, while she was filming *Interview with the Vampire*, Kirsten Dunst declared that kissing costar Brad Pitt was "like kissing your big brother—totally gross!" If you've ever said something you wish you hadn't...so what? That's in the past. If your words hurt a friend and it's not too late, you could try saying you're sorry. But often we agonize over things we said ages ago that don't matter anymore. If you have a mental drawer full of regrets, dump it and move on with your life. What matters most is what you say from now on.

TODADY
**I'll think before I say something
I might regret later.**

SOCIAL COMPETENCIES
ASSET #33: INTERPERSONAL COMPETENCE

December 20

*"It is often easier to fight for principles
than to live up to them."*
Adlai Stevenson

You insist you're not a racist, but when a friend
tells a racist joke, what do you do? You rant
about how bad stealing is, but when a clerk
gives you too much change, what do you do?
You're totally against cheating, but when someone offers you a copy of last year's history final,
what do you do? You probably know people
who say one thing and do another. Sometimes
they get away with it, sometimes they get
caught. Forget about them. What about you?

TODAY
I'll live up to my principles.

December 21

"One of the greatest gifts adults can give—
to their offspring and to their society—
is to read to children."

Carl Sagan

Many adults who love to read credit their parents for giving them that gift. They remember being read to as children. If you love to read—or even if you don't but would like to enjoy it more—spend time reading to a child. It might be your little sister or a neighbor child, or one child or a group at an elementary school (service project, anyone?), or the Saturday reading group at your public library. The kids will adore you, adults will appreciate you, and you'll feel good about yourself.

TODAY
I'll read to a child.

COMMITMENT TO LEARNING
ASSET #25: READING FOR PLEASURE

December 22

"Far away there in the sunshine are my
highest aspirations. I may not reach them,
but I can look up and see their beauty, believe
in them, and follow where they lead."

Louisa May Alcott

Marian Anderson wanted to sing in
Washington's Constitution Hall on Easter
Sunday, 1939, but she was barred because she
was black. So she gave her concert on the steps
of the Lincoln Memorial and drew a crowd of
75,000. Dr. Robert Jarvick was rejected by 15
American medical schools. He later invented an
artificial heart. History is full of people who
overcame obstacles on the way to achieving
their life purpose. Read their stories and be
inspired.

TODAY
I'll learn about people with purpose.

December 23

"Nobody succeeds beyond his or her wildest
expectations unless he or she begins
with some wild expectations."

Ralph Charell

Your parents want you to do *what?* Your track
coach thinks you can run *how* fast? Your
teacher says you should run for *that* student
office? When people believe in you, that's a sign
that maybe you're up to the task. Give it a try.
Or maybe there's something you've been aching
to do on your own—something that would surprise everyone, including you. Expectations are
powerful. They drive us to do and be our best.
If they come from the outside, that's great. If
they come from the inside, that's even better.

TODAY
I'll pursue a wild expectation.

BOUNDARIES AND EXPECTATIONS
ASSET #16: HIGH EXPECTATIONS

December 24

"I would draw a circle on a piece of paper
and my mother made me feel like Van Gogh."
Damon Wayans

Unless your parents are totally unsentimental
(or your family moves a lot), chances are there's
a box or drawer somewhere in your home that's
full of treasures. Not treasures to you, but
treasures to your mom and dad. They've kept
your preschool scribbles, that strange clay thing
you made in third grade, the birthday card you
drew on construction paper. The poem you
wrote. The video of your school concert. Any
trophy, award, or certificate you've ever won.
One look inside that box or drawer and your
parents get all misty.

TODAY
**I'll be thankful for my parents—
my biggest fans.**

December 25

*"Today, together, let us repeat
as our slogan that all trace of violence
must disappear from this earth."*
Monique Wittig

Take part in a national day of nonviolence. Join people across the country who are working for the common good. Meet people in your community who share your belief that peace is possible. Martin Luther King Jr. Day (the third Monday of January) has become a national day of service, interracial cooperation, and youth antiviolence initiatives. For more information, contact the Office of Public Liaison at the Corporation for National Service in Washington, D.C. (www.cns.gov). Or visit the Martin Luther King Jr. Day of Service Web site (www.mlkday.org).

TODAY
I'll plan to serve on Martin Luther King Jr. Day.

SOCIAL COMPETENCIES
ASSET #36: PEACEFUL CONFLICT RESOLUTION

December 26

*"My heroes are and were my parents.
I can't see having anyone else as my heroes."*
Michael Jordan

Many famous and successful people say their parents are their role models. They credit them with inspiring them, guiding them, being there for them, keeping them out of trouble, and teaching them to aim high. Are your parents your role models? Why or why not? (Try to see beyond any normal parent-and-teen conflicts you may be having right now.) What qualities do your parents have that you admire? In what ways do you hope you're like them someday? What's the one thing you respect most about them?

TODAY
I'll see my parents as role models.

December 27

"There is a crack in everything.
That's how the light gets in."
Leonard Cohen

So you're not perfect? Welcome to the human race. If you're trying to be perfect, stop. Perfectionism is a trap. It can make you fearful of taking risks or making mistakes. You may become super-competitive and self-critical. Perfectionists set unrealistic goals for themselves. They define their self-worth in terms of what they do instead of who they are. If you're stressed, anxious, and depressed much of the time, you may be a perfectionist. Try being average for a day. Let yourself be messy, late, incomplete, a little lazy. Relax and see how it feels.

TODAY
I'll like myself the way I am—complete with all my flaws.

POSITIVE IDENTITY
ASSET #38: SELF-ESTEEM

December 28

"In choosing a friend, go up a step."
Jewish proverb

The fact is, you will be influenced by your friends. No matter how strong you think you are or how unique you feel. Their tastes, their decisions, their likes and dislikes and attitudes will rub off on you. So why not aim high? Look around and identify people you respect and admire. Not because they're popular, but because they're good people. Then try to get to know them.

TODAY
I'll pick one person I'd like to know better.

December 29

"Tell me, what is it you plan to do
with your one wild and precious life?"

Mary Oliver

When 1,000 students ages 13–17 were asked to name the one thing they want most out of life, 27.7 percent said "happiness." There's nothing wrong with that. Why would anyone want to be unhappy? How would that change the world for the better? To be happy, try these suggestions from David G. Myers, author of *The Pursuit of Happiness:* Act happy. Get enough sleep. Exercise. Form close relationships and take care of them. Care for your soul. Studies show that actively ~~religious~~ *spiritual* people are happier and cope better with crises.

TODAY
I'll be happy.

POSITIVE IDENTITY
ASSET #39: SENSE OF PURPOSE

December 30

"I want to feel that I made choices
that empowered me as a human being.
My career is going to be here and gone.
But I'm always going to be a human being.
And I want to look myself in the mirror and say
that I was the human being I wanted to be."

Danny Glover

Are you the human being you want to be?
Maybe you're not there yet, but you're on the
way. You'll make choices today that will shape
the person you'll be tomorrow, 5 years from
now, even 50 years from now. Some choices can
have huge, life-changing consequences. Other
choices—asking a question, reading a book,
saying hi to someone at school—may seem triv-
ial but can lead you in new directions. Be aware
of the choices you make today, large or small.
Be sure they're your choices.

TODAY
I'll make good choices.

POSITIVE VALUES
ASSET #28: INTEGRITY

December 31

"The beginning is always today."
Mary Wollstonecraft

New Year's Eve. Time to celebrate. But first, before the party begins, spend a few minutes thinking back on the year that's ending. Maybe it was a good one. Maybe not so good. If you want, next year can be the best ever. A lot of what happens tomorrow and all the days after is up to you. Some people like to make New Year's resolutions. If you're one of them, try this: Don't start any with "I won't...." Start them all with "I will...."

TODAY
I'll begin.

POSITIVE IDENTITY
ASSET #40: POSITIVE VIEW OF PERSONAL FUTURE

Subjects Index

H

Sources Index

Assets Index

See pages x–xv for definitions of each asset.

About the Author

Pamela Espeland has written and coauthored many books for teens, children, and adults including *Stick Up for Yourself!*, *What Kids Need to Succeed*, *What Teens Need to Succeed*, *Making the Most of Today*, and *Making Every Day Count*.